Lost Civilization

DUCKWORTH DEBATES IN ARCHAEOLOGY
Series editor: Richard Hodges

Lost Civilization

THE CONTESTED ISLAMIC PAST
IN SPAIN AND PORTUGAL

James L. Boone

Duckworth

First published in 2009 by
Gerald Duckworth & Co. Ltd.
90-93 Cowcross Street, London EC1M 6BF
Tel: 020 7490 7300
Fax: 020 7490 0080
info@duckworth-publishers.co.uk
www.ducknet.co.uk

A catalogue record for this book is available
from the British Library

ISBN 978 0 7156 3568 1

Typeset by Ray Davies

Printed and bound in Great Britain by
CPI Antony Rowe, Chippenham and Eastbourne

Contents

List of figures

7

List of figures

1

Debates

The title of this book was inspired by a plenary lecture given by Miquel Barceló in March 1992 at a conference of medieval archaeologists in the hill-top castle town of Mértola, in the Lower Alentejo of Portugal. The focus of the conference was a then a relatively new but rapidly growing field in Spain and Portugal – the archaeology of al-Andalus: the brilliant Islamic civilization that rose and fell between the eighth and fifteenth centuries AD. Archaeologists from at least three generations were present. From the older generation were scholars such as Barceló and Cláudio Torres, political activists from the old Left whose careers had begun in the late sixties and early seventies, during the last years of the Salazar and Franco regimes, which ended within a year of each other in 1974 and 1975. Torres, an art historian, had in fact spent the last years of the Salazar regime in forced political exile in Romania and Morocco. Also present were archaeologists such as Sonia Gutiérrez and Arturo Morales, whose careers had developed entirely in the post-Franco era, and who were bringing contemporary archaeological techniques and theory to the study of Islamic Iberia.

Miquel Barceló delivered the opening plenary lecture in the Cine-Teatro Marques Duque, located on Mértola's single main thoroughfare along the Guadiana river. In the course of his talk, Barceló outlined the ideas that would shortly become incorporated into his famous call-to-arms article 'Quina arqueologia per al-Andalus?' (1993: 'What kind of archaeology for al-Andalus?'), which would later be published in three Iberian languages (Catalan, Castilian, Portuguese). However, he prefaced these ideas with opening some remarks that I have not yet seen in print, so I will need to paraphrase: 'What we are dealing with here,' he said, 'is a lost civilization. But it is not lost in some dense tropical jungle or some trackless desert. It is lost in our own historiography.'

*

There are a couple of ways in which al-Andalus can be regarded as a kind of 'lost civilization'. First and foremost, the Islamic civilization that flourished in the medieval period has been lost, as Barceló suggested, in a historiographic tradition that privileged the Latin Christian and Gothic tradition from late Roman times down to the present and downplayed the role of the brilliant civilization that rose and fell there between the eighth and twelfth centuries. More than once, in the course of explaining to a native Spanish or Portuguese person what it was I was doing as an archaeologist in their country, I have had the reply: 'Oh the Arabs – they were just foreigners.' In this sense, it is a civilization lost in a national narrative that has no place for it.

It is lost a second sense by way of its uniqueness. Spain and Portugal are the only nations in Europe with a substantial Muslim and specifically Arab past (only Sicily has a similar trajectory, and parts of southeastern Europe under Turkish rule). As such, Iberia in the Middle Ages doesn't 'fit in'. Too 'Eastern' for traditional European medievalists and too 'Western' for traditional Middle Easternists (Safran 2000), al-Andalus has remained the subject for specialists in a kind of nether world, neither European nor Middle Eastern, and catalogued by outsiders under the pejorative and anachronistic misnomer 'Moorish Spain'.

Until the past two or three decades, the Islamic period was indeed regarded in Iberian historiography as a kind of foreign occupation – an 'historical parenthesis', in Guichard's (1976: 24, 27) apt phrase – without lasting cultural or demographic effects on what was regarded as a core Hispanic or Visigothic and Hispano-Roman tradition. The popular view of this 'foreign

10

occupation' has been seen in much the same way as the French might view the Nazi occupation of France during the Second World War. The problem, of course, is that the Arab 'occupation' of Iberia lasted anywhere from four to seven hundred years – longer, in most cases, than Europeans have been in North America.

Throughout much of the nineteenth and twentieth centuries, the official cultures of Spain and Portugal were concerned with forging identities as modern nation states, on a par with the development of the rest of western Europe. The Arab invasion of 711 represented to them an interruption of 'normal' development characteristic of Latin Christian Europe north of the Pyrenees, diverting eternal Spain from its true destiny: if it weren't for the Arabs, Spain would be a modern nation of Europe like England or France (Kamen 2007: 91). The idea that for several centuries during the Middle Ages, not only had a majority of its population converted to Islam, but that the southern half of the Peninsula had become the seat of a brilliant independent, indigenous Islamic civilization, did not fit easily into this scheme of normal European development. That the Islamic period involved the introduction of a cultural and religious tradition that would become a kind of nemesis for Latin Christian culture for the next millennium did not make acceptance of an Islamic past any easier.

The traditionalist view that the Islamic period was fundamentally alien to Spain and Portugal's historical development has its beginnings not in the '*reconquista*' itself but in the late fifteenth century, nearly two hundred years after all the former Muslim territories but Granada had fallen to the Christians (Hillgarth 1985). Under the growing political dominance of Castile/León, and particularly during the reign of Fernando and Isabella (1479-1504), the historical role of the Goths (or Visigoths) in Spanish history underwent a significant revitalization. Much of this revitalization was inspired or supported by the revival of the works of Isidore of Seville (AD 560-636), a Hispano-Roman bishop who in 625 published a glowing and idealized *History of the Goths* (*Historia de Regibus Gothorum, Vandalorum et Suevorum*).

11

Isidore's narrative was unique among contemporary accounts of the Germanic groups that had built states in the former Roman colonies, in that rather than being a Romanized native's account of interlopers' foibles and excesses (as in Gregory of Tours' account of the Franks) or an insider's ethnic origin myth, as in Jordanes' *Getica*, the *Historia* was an outsider's attempt to forge a vision of the Visigoths as having been chosen by God to succeed Rome, to preserve and carry on the Christian faith, and perhaps most importantly, to unify the Iberian Peninsula under a single government. At the same time, Isidore was seen by contemporary Hispano-Romans as having been sent by God to save Hispanic civilization and the Roman Catholic tradition from the onslaughts of the Goths, largely by virtue of his successful campaign to convert the Visigoths from Arianism to Roman Catholicism, which he accomplished in 587-9, when he was apparently only 27 or 28 years old.

Isidore's vision of the Goths as carriers of Roman Christian tradition served Fernando and Isabella's purposes perfectly in their goal to unify the Peninsula under a single monarchy, a goal that was attained, albeit briefly, under Carlos V, when even Portugal lost its sovereignty to Castile. By the sixteenth century, the idea that there was a direct line leading from the Visigothic kings to the Hapsburg monarchs was the standard version of Spanish history. Isidore was canonized in 1598.

By the nineteenth/twentieth century, essentially two versions of Spanish and Portuguese medieval history had emerged (Butt 2007). One, a nationalist or conservative view, held that the Visigoths were heir to Christian Rome and that by the sixth/seventh century they already embodied the identity of the future Spanish nation. This identity was threatened by various intruders, including the Jews, but especially by the Arab Muslim invasion in 711. After centuries of crusading, the Spanish nation was restored in 1492 with the defeat of Granada and the expulsion of the Jews. The Inquisition was established to stave off further threats. An opposing view, a liberal, progressive, left-wing programme, sees the Islamic period as a time of tolerance and prosperity during which Christians, Jews and Muslims lived in relative harmony. The *reconquista* and the Inquisition that followed effectively destroyed this harmony and sent Spain off on a trajectory of economic decline and isolation. This multicultural society was derailed by the *reconquista* and ensuing Hispano-centric policies after 1492. This view found its most passionate and energetic proponent in Américo Castro (1885-1972), who in 1948 published *The Spaniards: An Introduction to Their History* while in exile in the United States. Castro argued that modern Spanish cultural identity came into being only during the Middle Ages as a result of a kind of 'dynamic tension' that existed between Christians, Muslims and Jews, which he called *convivencia*. In Castro's view, this dynamic tension was not necessarily friendly or peaceful, just stimulating and productive (Hillgarth 1985). However, the idea of *convivencia* in al-Andalus, today interpreted and perhaps over-idealized as a state of peaceful coexistence, has undergone a revival in post-Franco Spain. Its proponents (for example María Rosa Menocal in her glowing depiction of life in caliphal Córdoba, 2002) see al-Andalus as a potential model for Christian, Jewish and Muslim coexistence in an increasingly multicultural European Community.

It is probably fair to say that the conservative view of Spain's medieval past dominated historiography during the late nineteenth century and again particularly during the Franco regime up to 1975. Extended studies that dealt solely and specifically with the history and society of Muslim Spain were, almost needless to say, few and far between in Spain itself. Major studies of Muslim Spain that did appear were produced by European scholars outside Spain or Portugal, the majority of them in France, where there was a lively tradition of North African studies stimulated by France's colonial holdings there. Spain's colony in northern Morocco produced a few distinguished Arabists as well, most notably Ambrosio Huici Miranda. Very little archaeological work was devoted to the Islamic period outside such projects as the restoration of the Alhambra or an occasional 'Moorish bath', and most medieval archaeology in Spain during this time focused on 'Visigothic' churches and the large row-grave cemeteries excavated in the central Meseta (see Chapter 2). An interesting exception to this was the research into the history and archaeology of al-Andalus which was, significantly, sponsored by the French-supported and -funded Casa de Velázquez, founded in Madrid in 1928.

Such Spanish studies of the Islamic period as were produced and published typically found a way to accommodate the four to seven century Arab and North African dominion over Spanish culture into a narrative that was acceptable to the prevailing views. Francisco Javier Simonet's (1829-1897) monumental *Historia de los mozárabes de España* (1897-1903) argued that the Spanish Catholic tradition had been kept alive by the Spanish Mozarab minority (Christians who resisted conversion to Islam and remained in Muslim Iberia; see Chapter 3) throughout the Islamic period, emerging triumphant in the fourteenth to fifteenth centuries. A more typical response was what has become known as the 'traditionalist' view: that the vast majority of the population during the Islamic period was of indigenous origin and that Muslims entered the Peninsula slowly and in small numbers and were almost completely assimilated. After a few generations, the Muslim invaders had married into and allied with Hispano-Roman families and were 'Hispanicized'. Islam in al-Andalus was fundamentally 'Spanish' Islam. One of the most influential proponents of this view was Ramón Menendez Pidal, who even argued that the influence had gone the other way: the Spanish Hispanicized Islam! (Kamen 2007: 91).

The 'traditionalist' view in fact often differed radically from the official line in that it held that a Hispanic cultural substrate, with its own distinctive *mentalité*, had prevailed even since prehistory, absorbing or assimilating any and all alien characteristics, including Roman and Christian. Claudio Sanchez-Albornoz, for example, whose *Spain, An Historical Enigma* (1956), published in part as a riposte to Castro's vision of the medieval origins of the Spanish character, argued that a

1. Debates

Hispanic cultural and racial core had its origins in pre-Roman times and had remained more or less intact through a series of alien imperial expansionist episodes that included the Romans, the Visigoths, and finally the Muslims (Glick 1979: 7; Guichard 1976: 27). Sanchez-Albornoz had in fact been a member of the Republican government prior to the Civil War, and spent the entire Franco regime in exile, returning only after 1976.

One of the most extreme proponents of the traditionalist view was Ignacio Olagüe, who argued that the Muslim invasions as such never occurred, and that Hispanic peoples had adopted Islam voluntarily and independently to produce a distinctive, indigenous Andalusian Islamic culture and government in preference to the decadent Visigothic regime weakened by centuries of drought and plague and a corrupt, essentially polytheistic religious ideology; Islam represented a return to a pure form of monotheism. He argued that the first emir, Abd al-Rahman I, was actually a Visigothic renegade renamed by historians two or three centuries later in an attempt to invent an Arabic past for Spain. For Olagüe, the advent of Islamic dominion in Spain was a grassroots political and ideological revolution in a kind of Trotskian sense. Olagüe first published his book in France under the title *Les arabes n'ont jamais envahi l'Espagne* ('The Arabs never invaded Spain') in 1969, and it was republished in Barcelona in 1974 as *La revolución islámica en occidente* ('The Islamic revolution in the West'). It is only fair to point out that the scenario envisioned by Olagüe is not without historical precedent in the spread of Islam: Islamization in the Far East, particularly the Indonesian Archipelago, occurred entirely through proselytism by Muslim merchants, and Indonesia is presently the most populous Muslim country in the world. It is not, however, an Arab culture − that is, it did not adopt Arab language, culture and statecraft − as al-Andalus clearly did.

All these views of Spain's Islamic past finally boil down to some kind of subjective judgment involving a national narrative intent on recovering the 'essence' or 'meaning' of Spanish and Portuguese history. Documentary and archaeological data

15

can be adduced to prove that the Arabs did indeed invade the Iberian Peninsula when they said they did. But the idea that the Arabs were completely assimilated or 'Hispanicized', that the Hispanic race survived the several centuries long occupation 'intact', that the true origin of the Hispanic character lies in the Middle Ages, the Paleochristian Roman period, or the Iberian Iron Age, all involve some kind of subjective judgment that cannot be proved one way or the other. And, in fact, towards the end of the twentieth century this whole style of historiographical argumentation began to give way to a more objectively based, fact-oriented, observational kind of social history and archaeology. Consequently, the debate over the past 20 years or so has shifted to one concerned with the degree to which Islamic dominion in the Iberian Peninsula was a process of conquest, in-migration and demographic and cultural replacement or conversion, adoption and assimilation of Islamic culture and language by indigenous Hispano-Romans and Visigoths. 'Islamization' became the operative term. This kind of debate is a familiar one to European prehistorians, and the fact that a great deal of documentary evidence exists for this period will serve as a reminder that migration/independent adoption debates are not limited to prehistory, nor are they necessarily resolved by the presence of considerable historical documentation.

The Guichard hypothesis

In the mid-1970s, Pierre Guichard (1976) presented a sustained and detailed argument against the prevailing 'traditionalist' view of the Islamic period. Guichard was working in the *Annales* school of historiography, in which social groups and social formations are defined or informed by *mentalités* – modes of consciousness and representation in the past such that these mental models drive, or at least equilibrate, history. One of his earliest position statements was an article in *Annales* entitled 'Les arabes ont bien envahi l'Espagne' (1974: 'The Arabs certainly did invade Spain'). In a sense, Guichard and the Spanish

1. Debates

traditionalists were on opposite sides of the same coin. In order to justify continuity with an ancient Christian or Hispanic tradition, the traditionalists had to deny or minimize the importance of the Arabs' contribution to Spain's historical trajectory. On the other hand, in order to prove that the Islamic period was real, Guichard had to posit a radical shift or rupture in historical tradition. For this reason, perhaps, Guichard was forced to overstate his position concerning the nature and degree of rupture, a point to which I will return later in Chapters 4 and 6.

Drawing on structural-functionalist theory in social anthropology, Guichard argued that the Islamic and Latin Christian worlds were based on opposing structural principles of organization in the domestic domain, reflected in differences in systems of descent (patrilineal vs. bilineal), the organization of kin groups (corporate descent groups vs. bilateral kindreds), marriage patterns, the public role of women, and notions of honour. A more detailed account of this framework can be found in Goody (1984: 13-20), who ultimately calls into question the depth of the opposition between the two systems. Because the two systems were structurally opposed at a very basic level (i.e. at the level of the household), and because Arab and Berber principles of clan endogamy discouraged intermarriage with indigenous peoples, Guichard argues that very little in the way of acculturation or syncretization could have occurred. He further argued that the number of in-migrating Arabs and particularly North African Berbers was actually quite large, numbering in the hundreds of thousands, not the few tens of thousands envisioned by the traditionalists (1976: 456-7). Further, drawing on Murphy and Kasdan's (1959) analysis of Bedouin kinship and sociopolitical organization, Guichard argued that segmentary lineage organization facilitated the defence, expansion and growth of these groups at the expense of indigenous populations once they arrived in the Peninsula (1976: 257ff.). Thus Muslims became a demographic as well as a political and cultural majority in the Peninsula.

The publication of Guichard's work in the mid-1970s galva-

17

nized Islamic studies in the Iberian Peninsula, coinciding as it did with the end of the Franco and Salazar/Caetano regimes in Spain and Portugal, which had at least indirectly discouraged much serious or sustained historical or archaeological research into the Islamic period. A number of the major figures in Islamic archaeology and history that emerged in the years after 1975 came from the Left. But the effect of Guichard's work was more than a political coincidence. Guichard's model lent itself particularly well to verification using archaeological data (see below and Chapter 4). It redefined the entire field of inquiry and it made the archaeology of al-Andalus broadly comparable with early medieval archaeology in the rest of Europe. With its emphasis on family structure and social organization as the basic building blocks of civilization, it transformed historical archaeology into an anthropological endeavour. In a field dominated by a focus on monuments, castles and urban settlements, it provided a rationale for archaeological research into rural settlement, including household archaeology, village organization and rural settlement patterns. Finally, and most importantly, Guichard's model points to the importance of the implantation of rural social and settlement patterns – patterns that are for the most part invisible in written documents. It thus changed the role of archaeological research from one of verification and illustration of already established historical 'facts' to one in which archaeological evidence becomes a primary, and in many cases, the sole source of evidence in historical interpretation.

Hence, the effect of Guichard's ideas was particularly strong in the rapidly developing field of Iberian Islamic archaeology, and perhaps nowhere in the world has historical archaeology played a more pivotal role in the rewriting of a nation's social and cultural history (Glick 1995: xii-xvii). By the early 1980s, Belgian and French archaeologists André Bazzana and Patrice Cressier, working with Guichard, attempted to operationalize Guichard's hypothesis concerning the cultural and demographic processes by which Islamic culture became implanted on the Iberian cultural landscape by focusing on the relationship between castles – termed *husun* (sing. *hisn*) in Arabic – and the surrounding hinterland composed of small villages called *alquerías* (from the Arabic *al-qarya*, for village). Their programme of research into the *hisn/qarya* complex was largely inspired by Pierre Toubert's (1973; 1990) concept of *incastellamento*: a term which refers to the reorganization of European settlement in the ninth to eleventh centuries around hilltop fortifications, or castles, which imposed feudal dominance on dependent villages within their jurisdiction. However, in contrast to northern Europe and Italy, where *incastellamento* refers to a system in which hinterlands were organized and controlled by a seigniorial (i.e. feudal) regime, Bazzana, Cressier and Guichard view the Iberian *hisn/qarya* complex as the expression of the egalitarian, segmentary tribal organization that is a key element of Guichard's original hypothesis concerning how Islamic culture became established in Iberia. Under this system, the inhabitants of the *alquerías* were free of any feudal-like obligations to a regional lord or *qaid*, and held and farmed lands collectively. The *hisn*, in turn, was, at least in the earliest centuries of the medieval period, a fortified refuge built and maintained by the tribal collectives as protection in times of disorder, not as a means of implementation of control by a higher authority. Bazzana, Cressier and Guichard extensively documented the *hisn/qarya* complex in the Levantine Peninsula particularly in the areas around Valencia, Alicante and Almería (Bazzana et al. 1988; Bazzana et al. 1982; Cressier 1991; 1992).

The medieval transition

Guichard's programme was subsequently subjected to several kinds of criticisms, discussed in more detail in Chapter 4, but the main problem has been that it does not tell us much about what happened to the several million people – probably somewhere between three and five million – who were living in the Peninsula at the time of the first invasions in AD 711, or how they were incorporated into Islamic society. Certainly a great deal of the Islamization of Iberian society and culture can be explained in terms of conversion of indigenous Hispano-Romans and Visigoths (Bulliet 1979). Christians are known to have emigrated to the northern Christian-dominated territories of the Peninsula, particularly by the ninth and tenth centuries. Jews, on the other hand, appear to have actually benefited from Muslim dominion relative to the harsh anti-Semitic policies of the Visigoths, and may have even assisted in the conquest. But it is clear that Islamization, if that is what we want to call it, played out over a period of several hundred years following the initial invasions. Furthermore, how and how rapidly the process played out varied widely in its nature from region to region, and was contingent upon variable environmental, demographic, economic and political conditions. And finally, and perhaps most importantly, neither the material nor the documentary record reflect a total replacement of peoples, cultures, structural principles, or anything else, but rather a melding of elements from both cultures to produce a distinctively Andalusian society. Nowhere is this clearer than in the archaeological record of the first few centuries of Arab dominion, as I shall discuss in more detail in Chapter 5.

Consequently, many Spanish archaeologists have adopted the idea of the early medieval period as a 'transitional' period, following the lead of archaeologists of the early medieval period elsewhere on the European sub-continent (Gutiérrez Lloret 1996: 17-24). Earlier formulations of the 'medieval transition' model emphasized the origins of Christian institutions in late antiquity, institutions that would come to dominate the European cultural landscape by the eighth and ninth centuries, and which continue into the modern period (e.g. the work of Peter Brown 1971; 1978). While certainly applicable to the Visigothic period in Iberia, this view of the transition would not seem to have much relevance for the Islamic period. However, the work of the historian Chris Wickham (Wickham 1984; 1985; 2005) cast the problem of the medieval transition in much more general terms, and into terms that turned out to be very 'user friendly' for archaeologists.

1. Debates

For Wickham, the problem of the medieval transition concerns all of the lands previously under the dominion of the Roman empire, and what happened to them following the dissolution of the empire (2005:10-12). Thus, the transition occurred on all sides of the Mediterranean world and on the European subcontinent, regardless of whether the end result was a Muslim culture and society or a Latin Christian one. It is admittedly a Romano-centric way of looking at the problem. It is certainly worth pointing out that from the point of view of the Islamic world, there is nothing 'medieval' about this particular segment of time: it is the classical period, the period of beginnings. Wickham has in fact, attempted to extend his formulation to lands outside the former Roman empire (1985). In any case, the Romano-centric approach does provide a sound basis for comparison and analysis of regional variation in the former Roman world.

In his landmark 1984 article, 'The Other Transition', Wickham argued that one of the problems with characterizing what changed between the end of the Roman empire and the emergence of feudalism is that some institutions that seem distinctly medieval – such as seigniorial land tenure – had already existed in late antiquity, and that similarly, institutions that seem to belong to Rome persisted well into the medieval period. Wickham's proposal was that the transition between antiquity and the medieval world can be interpreted fundamentally in terms of a shift in the manner in which surplus was extracted from primary agricultural producers. In late antiquity, the dominant mode of surplus extraction was in the form of a land tax. By the medieval period, the balance had gradually shifted toward surplus extraction in the form of rent. From this deceptively simple formula can be extrapolated many of the salient material, institutional and ideological features of antiquity and its decline, and the emergence of the medieval world.

The centralized land tax system had been the principal source of funding for the late Roman state apparatus. It financed the city of Rome and the provincial cities that formed

21

the basis of the empire's 'cellular' structure. It paid the central administration and the army, which protected the lands in the provinces and made it possible for wealthy patricians to own lands in several provinces. It financed the construction of monumental public architecture. It paid for the far-flung postal system that maintained communication between the provinces. It supported state workshops in arms and textiles. Finally, the tax system both underwrote and stimulated long-distance trade, which moved staples from the provinces to Rome and distributed luxuries and household material goods back to the provinces. Taxes paid in money provided the capital for the construction of ships, ports and roads, and financed the trade ventures themselves. The tax system stimulated that trade in the sense that farmers in the provinces had to intensify production in order to raise money to pay the taxes.

The Roman state apparatus for collecting taxes evaporated rather suddenly over much of western Europe in the first few decades of the fifth century, most proximally as a result of the withdrawal of the military from the western colonies. The barbarian states that took their place, such as the Franks and the Visigoths, continued to use the Roman model to collect taxes into the seventh century, but for Wickham, at least, centralized tax collection becomes increasingly marginal to the political economy of the early middle ages (Wickham 2005: 99-100). For the Visigothic kings, taxes formed the basis for a kind of personal slush-fund, and the kings become increasingly alienated from the upper nobility; this ultimately was the central weakness of the Visigothic state. Díaz (2000) has pointed to a growing disconnection between cities and the countryside. In antiquity the cities were the centres of tax collection, investing a portion locally in urban development and sending the rest on to Rome. By the late Roman period, cities functioned mainly as cultic centres, under the control of bishops. In the hinterlands, rural landholders developed ties of dependency with their tenant producers, and maintained their own private protection, with rent paid in kind more often than in coin. Hence, in Wickham's words, we see the 'translation of public obligations [i.e. taxes] into relationships of personal dependence, and the association of these with landholding' (2005: 99).

Since the Arab emirate and caliphate in al-Andalus were without question tax collecting entities, this might seem difficult to reconcile with Wickham's tax-to-rent formula, but he has devised an ingenious argument around this problem, inspired in large part by the ideas of Eduardo Manzano Moreno (Wickham 2005: 97-102; see below). Because the landholding and surplus extracting elites of Hispania were dispersed throughout the countryside rather than concentrated in the cities, the Arab conquerors were forced to adapt their system of tax collection to this new social and political landscape. Since the new state could not collect taxes fast enough, they had to pay their army with land instead, creating a class of mostly Arabized Berber landholders, called *baladiyyun*, at the very outset. Furthermore, as a result of the dispersed nature of landholdings, tax collection had to be farmed out to detachments of soldiers (such as the *junds*, discussed in more detail in Chapter 3), who were granted concessions to collect taxes from a given locality. This system of collection is called the *iqta'*, or tax farming (Cahen 1953; see Wickham 1985 for a discussion of how the transition scheme fits the East). The extent to which tax farming played a role in early al-Andalus is poorly understood, but seems likely to have been important. The collectors would keep part of the tax as pay and forward the rest to the state. Although theoretically they did not own the land worked by the taxpayers, it seems likely that over time, they would have developed ties of personal dependence with their tax-payers that resemble those of feudal Europe (I discuss this issue in more detail in Chapter 4). In yet other cases, the conquerors allowed resident landholding elites to retain the lands and tenants they controlled, collecting taxes through them, as in the case of the Visigoth Theodemir, who held a fiefdom in southeastern Spain at the time of the conquest, which became the *kura*, or district, of Tudmir under Arab rule (Gutiérrez Lloret 1996; see Chapter 3 of this book).

In any case, the application of Wickham's model of the medieval transition to Islamic Spain has had the inclusive effect of bringing al-Andalus into the comparative picture with the rest of the medieval world, and thus resolving the problem of 'uniqueness' that I alluded to at the beginning of this chapter. This is all the more true because Wickham's model is amenable to archaeological testing: he has worked closely with archaeologists – particularly in northern Italy – since the 1980s (Randsborg 1989) and he incorporates archaeological data into his work as primary data on a par with documentary evidence, rather than simply as props to illustrate already established historical facts, patterns and events.

Finally, the recent publication in 2006 of Eduardo Manzano Moreno's *Conquistadores, emires y califas* has signalled a subtle but decisive shift in the historiography of the Islamic period in Spain. The title of the book itself suggests the shift: the Arabs not only invaded Hispania, they conquered it. This shifts the focus of explanation away from the Iberian Peninsula in particular to the Arab empire in general – that is, the problem becomes how and under what conditions the Arabs imposed their rule over Hispania, taking into account the particular problems that the pre-conquest structure of the Iberian landscape posed to Arab state builders in al-Andalus. Manzano Moreno's approach draws inspiration from the pioneering scholarship of Patricia Crone (1980; 1987) in her work on the formation and organization of the expanding Arab empire in the East. In Spain, signs of this broadened comparative approach can be found as far back as 1994, with the publication of Pedro Chalmeta's (1994b) *Invasion e islamización* and Peter Scales' *The Fall of the Caliphate of Córdoba* (1994), several foundational articles by Maribel Fierro (1995a; b; 1999; for a good English language introduction to her ideas see Fierro 2005), the collection of articles by Miquel Barceló in *El sol que salió por occidente* (1997b), and the publication by the Casa de Velázquez of *Genèse de la ville islamique en al-Andalus et au Maghreb occidental* (Cressier & García-Arenal 1998).

Under this approach, one of the key issues of debate centres around tribalism and the state, and in particular, the degree to which tribalism played a continuing role in the formation of al-Andalus. One view, pioneered by Guichard, but further developed by the historian and linguist Miquel Barceló (see in particular 1990; although his views differ in important ways from Guichard's), is that Arabs and Berbers entered the Peninsula organized as segmentary lineages and retained this organization for at least several centuries following the invasion. Furthermore, the tribal nature of social organization in the hinterlands is essential to understanding the particular nature of the formation of the Andalusian state. A second view, argued most recently by Manzano Moreno (2006: 129-53), is that Arabs and Berbers may have at one time been characterized by this kind of tribal organization but that it rapidly broke down as they settled under new circumstances in al-Andalus, such that it is of relatively minor importance in understanding the structure of Andalusian society. Manzano Moreno and others argue that the most important social unit is the *faction*, a group of individuals united by common interests, and who may have varying ethnic origins. I will discuss this issue in more detail in Chapter 4.

*

This book, which takes the form of an extended essay, is intended as an introduction for English language readers to recent and current debates regarding the transition between late antiquity and medieval Islamic Spain and Portugal, as seen from the point of view of an archaeologist. While my discussion of the relevant historical debates in relation to the archaeology is based entirely on secondary sources, I have attempted to rely on primary publications in my discussion of the archaeological evidence whenever possible. Several biases will become evident. My own work on the medieval period in the Iberian Peninsula has been in the region around Mértola, in the Lower Alentejo of Portugal, where I have worked with the Campo Arqueológico de Mértola team since 1988 (preceded by several years in northern Morocco with Charles L. Redman).

Hence I will include rather more material on this little corner of the Peninsula than is usually found in discussions such as this one. This isn't such a bad thing, because this region has some important things to tell us, particularly about that hazy period between the sixth and the ninth centuries. My work has been almost entirely concerned with small rural villages, so I will be talking about those quite a lot. But I am not alone in thinking that rural settlement research has been underemphasized. I am one out of what seems to be less than a handful of American archaeologists working in this area, rightfully dominated by European researchers. So this is bound to put an odd kind of spin on my discussion, but perhaps I am not the best person to be the judge of that.

2

The background of late antiquity

The *Hispania* of late antiquity, and more precisely that of the end of the fifth century until the beginning of the eighth, presents an historical, cultural, economic and social picture very similar to the rest of the provinces of the by then defunct Roman empire. Despite its being at the westernmost end of the known world, its pattern of historical development fits directly in the context of Mediterranean and European history. (Ripoll López & Velázquez 1995: 6)

The idea that the Iberian Peninsula had been on a historical trajectory in line with Europe north of the Pyrenees until it was, for better or for worse, depending on one's politics, knocked off course forever by the Arab invasion has been a powerful one in Hispanic historiography. Iberia was the first region of western Europe to be incorporated into the Roman empire, and was perhaps the most thoroughly Romanized – certainly it was the most urbanized region of western Europe during the empire. Roman political and military control of Iberia evaporated at about the same time as in Gaul and Britain, that is, during the first decade or two of the fifth century. At about this time, a succession of mostly northern European groups entered the Peninsula, predominantly the Sueves, a mixed group consisting of Vandals, Alans and Visigoths. The Vandals and Alans stayed only about 20 years, and then crossed over to North Africa to found a state centred on Carthage, which is now Tunisia. Of the two main groups that stayed, the Visigoths emerged supreme, defeating the Sueves

Period	Date AD	Characterization
Late Roman	409-711	Disappearance of Roman imperial state apparatus. Continuation of Roman cultural and settlement traditions. Control of Peninsula by Visigothic and Byzantine interests.
Conquest	711-756	Initial Arab and Berber invasions from North Africa. al-Andalus administered by a governor (*wali*), as a district of Ifriqya (North Africa). Arrival of the Syrian *junds* (military units) in 740s. Fall of Umayyad dynasty in Damascus in 750, replaced by the Abbasids.
Emiral	756-929	Arrival in 756 of Umayyad refugee Abd al-Rahman I, the first *emir*, who effectively declares al-Andalus an independent state. Crisis, fragmentation from the mid-800s to the early 900s. Increasing cultural dominance of Islam.
Califal	929-1009	Unification of al-Andalus under the Umayyad caliphate, centered in Córdoba. Construction of *Madinat al-Zahra* as a separate palace city from Córdoba.
Taifal	1009-1140s	Caliphate breaks up into a series of independent city-states called *taifas* Christian kingdoms along the Marches make significant advances (1080s).
North African	1086-1250	al-Andalus falls under Almoravid (1086-1106), then Almohad (1145-1250) control; a second *taifa* period, political fragmentation, unrest in the 1140s. Centre of power shifts to Seville.
Nasrid	1230-1492	Córdoba falls to the Christians in 1236, Seville in 1246. Nasrid kingdom of Granada.

Table 2.1. Chronology of the late Roman and Islamic period in the Iberian Peninsula.

and incorporating them into their polity in 584. As we saw in the previous chapter, the Visigoths have been seen as the key link between the Roman Christianity of late Roman Spain (the Paleochristian period) and the unified Catholic nation that emerged in the later Middle Ages, after the final defeat of Granada in 1492.

Views of the Visigoths – who they were and what their role was in the development of early medieval Spain – have undergone a near complete revolution over the past few decades. The traditional 'Migration Period' narrative holds that the Goths left their homeland in Scandinavia sometime in the third century, crossed the Baltic and settled in what is now Pomerania. Subsequently, they first expanded south to the north and west shores of the Black Sea, then west into southern Gaul, and finally south into the Iberian Peninsula, maintaining all the while their primordial tribal cohesion and ancient clan organization, and remaining throughout a distinct ethnic and perhaps genetic entity as well. More generally, the Germanic tribes were seen as a comprising a more or less homogeneous, even monolithic 'civilization' across the Rhine and the Danube, so that following the invasions, this Germanic civilization was transplanted onto former Roman lands and transformed antique culture into a new and distinctly medieval one (Collins 2004; Goffart 2006). Under this view, the assumption that the Goths might carry with them a distinct and persistent archaeologically visible signature as well was not unreasonable.

More recently, under the 'ethnogenesis' view developed originally by Viennese historians Pohl and Reimitz (1998), the Goths have been seen more as roving armies and refugees, composed perhaps predominantly of males brought in from diverse ethnic backgrounds. These roving groups were organized around and ruled by a core ethnic elite termed a *Traditionskern*, or core tradition, which essentially fostered and furnished a kind of 'constructed' ethnic identity for the whole motley group and maintained a real or fabricated historical tradition of their origins and wanderings from ancestral homelands. The capacity to become a king or a magnate would be contingent upon membership in the ethnic elite. Such groups entered Europe initially under the service of the remnants of the Roman empire as *foederati*. Under this view, the proportion of the group who were ethnically Gothic was presumably rather smaller than envisioned under the traditional view, and there is less of an expectation that they carried with them a distinct, homogeneous material culture that would serve as an archaeological signal of their distinct ethnicity.

There has also been a major shift in views about how and in what role the migrating 'tribes' settled in Romanized and Christianized Europe. Under the traditional view, the Visigoths who settled under the institution of *hospitalitas*, for example in southern Gaul, did so with the assent of the Roman authorities, and received a third of the property in a given province in return for military service, while two-thirds remained with Roman estate owners. Later the portions seem to have reversed, and the barbarians took two-thirds (Halm 1998; Wolfram 1987: 222-4). In any case, the arrangement was seen as a kind of compromise designed to mollify the barbarian invaders. In 1980, the historian Walter Goffart (1980) offered a novel reinterpretation of *hospitalitas*. Rather than land, Goffart argued that the Roman provincials offered the barbarians a portion of the tax revenues, which they were charged with collecting, along with the right to settle (see a revision and reinforcement of this view in Goffart 2006: ch. 6 and passim). As we will see in Chapter 4, this system bears a strong resemblance to the system of tax farming practised in the expanding Arab empire, a practice that may have its origins in Byzantine statecraft.

Furthermore, the militarization of late antique and early medieval culture was seen as a trend originating and intensifying in the Roman empire itself, having already begun in the third century (Brown 1971: 24-9) rather than being imposed by the barbarians. The emerging military hierarchy becomes a vehicle for barbarian upward social mobility, while the ecclesiastical hierarchy, which required extended religious and philological training from an early age, remains largely the domain of Romanized natives of the former colonies. The barbarians thus become stakeholders in Roman civilization rather than just marauders or destroyers, as well as participants in the formation of a new kind of society – a medieval one – based on a dual power structure focused around a secular military elite headed by kings and counts, and a Christian ecclesiastical structure headed by bishops. This is not to say that the arrival of groups from north and east of the Rhine and the Danube did not cause considerable conflict and disruption of formerly secure avenues of trade, commerce and movement, as Ward-Perkins (2005) has forcefully argued. The point is, however, the incoming tribes were intent not necessarily on destroying the empire but rather somehow becoming a part of it and benefiting from it. In any case, by the time the Visigoths became players in the late Roman world of Hispania, they had already been incorporated into a territorial state in Aquitaine for nearly a century.

The Visigoths in Spain

On the basis of documentary evidence, the Visigoths first appear in the Iberian Peninsula in the early 400s, when they were sent from Gaul as a military force to unseat a Suevi leader who had installed himself at Seville (Bonnassie 1991b; Collins 2004; Ripoll López 1998). But the main population movement from Gaul must have occurred anywhere from sixty to a hundred years later. Certainly the fall of the Visigothic kingdom of Toulouse after the battle of Vouillé in 507 must have precipitated a mass movement of people into the Iberian Peninsula. The earliest archaeological evidence attributable to the Visigothic presence, mostly in the form of items of dress associated with burials, dates to this period.

Estimates as to number of immigrants vary from 80,000 to 200,000 with the mode of agreement centering around 100,000. Ripoll López (1998), in a projection based on the number and size of rural cemeteries and estimated urban populations, settles on a figure of 130,000, or about 20,500 families or households. However, of these, she suggests only 7,000 to

10,000, or about 1,500 families, comprised the military and landed aristocracy of the Peninsula (1998: 161). Meanwhile, estimates of the population of resident Hispano-Romans at the time of the Visigothic migration vary between three and five million, down from a peak of seven million during the height of the empire (Chalmeta 1994a). Using the 100,000 figure, then, the Visigothic population would likely have comprised only somewhere between 2% and 3.3% of the total population of the Peninsula; doubling the number of Visigoths would not appreciably increase their proportional representation. For those who doubt that late antiquity was characterized by decline in population, increasing the number of resident Hispano-Romans would dilute the Visigoths even more. There is not much reason to think that their numbers would have increased much, either absolutely or proportionally during the following two centuries, particularly in view of the recent evidence for a series of plague pandemics that begin in 541 and last until about 750 (Kulikowski 2007; Little 2007).

Visigothic settlement

The term 'Visigothic Spain', used ubiquitously to refer to the period between the early fifth century and 711, implies that Visigothic hegemony dominated the Iberian cultural landscape through these two-and-a-half to three centuries and that Visigoth dominance characterized the entire Peninsula definitively and homogeneously. And yet almost no one anymore freely accepts that either of these propositions even approaches the real situation. Olmo Enciso (1992) has categorized what he sees as the essential heterogeneity of the Peninsula during the period into three main areas. The first is the Mediterranean littoral, extending from the mouth of the Ebro through the Strait of Gibraltar to the Guadalquivir delta and beyond to the Algarve coast of Portugal, a region that was until the late sixth century under direct Byzantine control, including for several decades the cities of Córdoba and Seville. The second is central zone, consisting mainly of the central *meseta*, which encom-

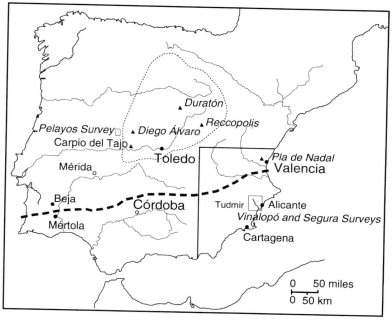

Fig. 2.1. Map of the Iberian Peninsula, showing cities, sites and areas discussed in the text. The area in the centre delimited by a dotted line contains the highest density of Visigothic period row-grave cemeteries, and is argued to be the principal area of Visigothic settlement. The heavy dotted line along the southern and eastern littoral indicates areas under Byzantine influence or direct control during the sixth century.

passes the early Visigothic capitals Mérida and Toledo, as well as the Visigothic royal city of Reccopolis. This is also the area of concentration of the debated row-grave 'Visigothic' cemeteries, discussed below. The third region, which is out of our area of concern for this book, is the Cantabrian and Galician coast down to the Douro river in northern Portugal, which encompasses the never-romanized territory of the Basques as well as the kingdom of the Sueves up to their defeat in 584. The southern and eastern fringes of this region in León would become the staging area for the expansion of Christian forces into al-Andalus during the so-called *reconquista*. Below, I discuss archaeological evidence that contributes to our understanding of the diversity in settlement and culture that existed in early medieval Hispania.

The central Meseta

The Meseta cemeteries. The row-grave cemeteries of the central and northern Meseta were long considered to be the most concrete evidence of Visigothic settlement (Reinhardt 1945; Palol 1966). About 70 cemeteries are known, most of which are distributed along the upper tributaries of the Tajo and especially the Duero rivers; an additional few are found along the upper Ebro, Guadiana, and Guadalquivir (Fig. 2.1). Several of these cemeteries have extensively excavated, the most well-known of which are the sites of Duratón and Carpio del Tajo. The Duratón cemetery is located about 120 km directly north of Madrid on a terrace above the Duratón river, a tributary that flows north into the Duero. The cemetery contains about 660 burials containing about 1,000 bodies. El Carpio del Tajo, consisting of 285 excavated burials, is located on a terrace above the Tajo river near the village of the same name about 40 km directly west of Toledo (Ripoll López 1985).

The character and meaning of row-grave, or *reihengraber*, cemeteries have been the focus of debate since the late 1970s. James (1979) was the first to argue that, contrary to previous assumptions, the Frankish row-graves are not necessarily reflective of areas of Frankish settlement *per se*, pointing out that the row-grave form of burial has no precedent in the presumed Frankish homeland north of the Rhine, and that the cemeteries are not even strongly correlated with demonstrably new Frankish settlements, but rather with old Gallo-Roman ones. He does argue, however, that the row-graves most likely reflect the establishment of a new Frankish landed aristocracy, and that the new orderly arrangement of graves with their Frankish style goods result from the adoption by dependants and tenants of the fashions of their Frankish lords. These dependants could have been both Frankish and Gallo-Roman. This is essentially the argument taken with regard to the Visigothic row-graves

2. The background of late antiquity

by Ripoll López (1998; 1999) and by Peter Heather (1996) in his survey of Gothic settlement.

Carpio del Tajo was excavated in the 1920s by Cayetano de Mergelina (1890-1962), a medieval archaeologist. The site was later completely destroyed, and in fact its exact location is no longer clear, but Mergelina left detailed notes and a plan of the burials, which Ripoll López reanalyzed in the 1980s. A total of 285 burials are recorded. Ripoll López (1998) argues that the cemetery was founded sometime between 490 and 525 with a foundational nucleus of well-furnished graves on the highest part of the site. The burials then expand north and south from this nucleus throughout the sixth century. During this time, burials with Roman objects start to appear in some graves, which Ripoll López suggests is evidence that Romans and Visigoths were being interred in the cemetery together without any spatial segregation. Finally, in the seventh century, burials continued to be added to the cemetery by infilling between earlier graves. Throughout the period of use, earlier burials were respected (i.e. not disturbed by later interments), so that surface grave markers must have been present. Ripoll López and Heather ultimately see the cemetery as reflective of a rural community of Visigoths and Romans perhaps united by land-lord-peasant ties of dependency.

Burials of men contain few grave goods or items of dress that would distinguish between Visigothic and Hispano-Roman identity. The graves lack weapons of any kind, a pattern that Heather (1996), as others before him, sees as characteristic of Gothic burials back through several centuries of movement from their apparent homeland around the mouth of Vistula river in Pomerania. Row-graves in the Frankish region of central and northern France, in contrast, commonly contain weapons such as swords and battle-axes. A portion of the burials of women at Carpio del Tajo, comprising about 20% of all the graves, were buried dressed in what Peter Heather has referred to the 'Danubian' style: 'a cloak held with a pair of fibula brooches at each shoulder, and large plated belt buckle around the waist' (1996: 202). The fibulae and buckles date to approximately 480/90 to 560/80. Heather traces this particular form of women's costume back to the third- and fourth-century Chernjachov culture north of the Black Sea and ultimately to the first- and second-century Wielbark culture at the mouth of Vistula river in Pomerania, an ancestry which he argues maps onto the historical movements of the Goths from their point of origin. Ripoll López, for her part, sees the pattern as reflective of the inheritance practice in which the 'moveable part of the dowry or *ornamenta muliebria* ... was exclusively part of the woman's property and not part of what was known as the "Family patrimonial community" ' (1998: 177).

Pizarras. The *pizarras* of the Spanish meseta are a remarkable and almost unique form of documentary evidence for the Dark Ages (Velázquez Soriano 2001). They are written documents scratched onto approximately page-sized leaves of slate that was quarried and shaped for that purpose. The content of these documents takes a variety of forms, including bills of sale, deeds to land, legal edicts, and harvest accounts. *Pizarras* are typically found associated with what appear to be habitation sites of estate or farm owners. The best known and most productive site has been the Lancha de Trigo locality near the village of Diego Álvaro located about midway between Salamanca and Avila. The site has produced several dozen of these stone documents. There is little information available, however, about the houses or settlements with which these documents were associated. An amazing range of information has been gleaned from the inscriptions from the fact that estate owners grew strawberries and made cider to the way that land was inherited and sold among relatives (Ripoll López & Velázquez 1995: 91-2, 116). The texts are in Latin, written in a cursive hand, and reflect a population in which at least some members were literate. They do not tell us anything directly about the ethnic identity of the makers or users.

Many of the texts contain dates or mention a Visigothic king, so that an approximate date can be assigned to the document. The handwriting styles of the texts can also be tied generally to a chronology. Of 151 texts published in Velázquez Soriano

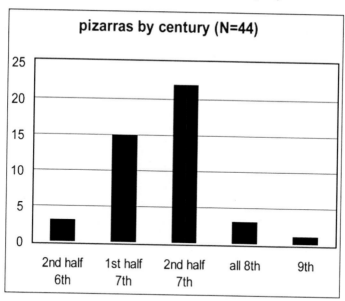

Fig. 2.2. Histogram showing the changing frequency of *pizarras* through time, based on those published in Velázquez Soriano (2001). Only slates that could be dated to a half-century were used (N = 44).

(2001) that can be generally dated to within a century, 44 can be specifically tied to half-century intervals. The histogram in Fig. 2.2 presents the temporal distribution of these 44 examples. This distribution shows that most of the texts date to the seventh century, and that there is a slight increase in the production of texts from 650 to 700, followed by an abrupt decline, obviously precipitated by the Arab conquest. Although the sample size is small, the increase in the second half of the seventh century does not speak to any notable decline in the production of these texts, or their makers.

Rural settlement on the Meseta. A site survey and excavations carried out by Francisco Fabian and others (Fabian et al. 1986) in the mid-1980s around the construction of a reservoir about 40 km south of Salamanca offer a glimpse of what Visigothic rural settlement was like on the northern Meseta. The survey area is located about midway between the Duero and Tajo rivers along a now mostly inundated irrigated section of the valley formed by the Rio Tormes which flows north and eventually empties into the Duero. The survey area is in turn about 45 km west of the site Diego Álvaro, discussed above. The area under investigation, approximately 80 by 30 km, surrounds the Santa Teresa reservoir, and reveals a scatter of Late Roman and Visigothic settlements, recognized on the basis of the presence or absence of late *terra sigillata*, plainware pottery, and *tegula* style roof tiles. Numerous *pizarras* have been recovered in the area, mostly within present-day villages that were formerly Visigothic period sites, including one bearing the name of Égica, the Visigothic king who ruled from 687 to 701.

Fabian et al. focused their investigation on the *dehesa* of Cañal, in the vicinity of Salvatierra de Tormes, which seems to have to have been the largest community in the region during Visigothic times. Here, the site of Cuartos de las Hoyas produced a series of structures dating to the fifth to seventh century (Fig. 2). These structures strongly resemble barns and animal pens maintained up to the present day and used to keep sheep, cattle and pigs. Fairly abundant pottery was recovered. Storage jars and cooking pots tend to reflect continuity with later Roman period forms. Also present are serving wares, including serving plates as well as Paleochristian or Visigothic style stamped bottles or cruets (*estampillado*) that were used to dispense liquids such as wine or oil. *Estampillado* is designated as 'Visigothic' pottery throughout the Peninsula, but the same kinds of floral and curvilinear stamped designs are found on wheel or slow wheel made bottles in Frankish Gaul, so this form of decorated pottery may more accurately be thought of as Late Roman, rather than specifically Visigothic or Frankish. The presence of cooking and serving ware in turn indicates a habitation somewhere in the vicinity of these structures, though nothing that looks especially like a house can be found in walls that were uncovered at Cuartos de las Hoyas. Other artifacts recovered from the site are *pizarras*, and metal arti-

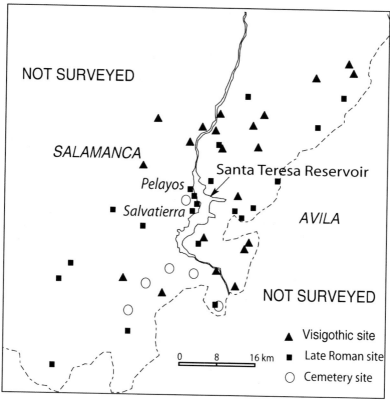

Fig. 2.3. Map of the Pelayos survey area around the Santa Teresa Reservoir area (Fabian et al. 1986). Late Roman sites are generally dated to the fourth to sixth century, and Visigothic sites are assigned to the sixth and seventh centuries, although there may well be some overlap.

facts, including an iron stylus that may have been used to engrave *pizarras*, and a bronze ring with a cross and possibly some initials.

A fragment of an engraved bronze belt buckle, typically found in graves of the Visigothic period, may indicate the presence of a small cemetery near this settlement, although no actual tombs were found here. Tombs with slate covering stones have been found within a kilometre of the site.

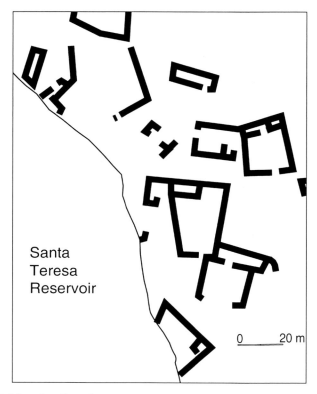

Fig. 2.4. Map of walls and structures uncovered at the Pelayos site on the edge of the Santa Teresa Reservoir (Fabian et al.1986).

Although much work remains to be done to fill in the details, the settlement pattern around Santa Teresa reservoir and the excavations at the Cañal at least allow us to piece together a hypothetical picture of what Late Roman and Visigothic settlement and settlement systems may have been like in the Meseta during the two or three centuries before the Arab conquest. Some or even most of the sites identified as Late Roman in the survey described by Fabian et al. may have been abandoned by the sixth to seventh centuries, but it is tempting to see in this distribution a dispersed pattern of farming, or more specifi-

40

cally, ranching settlements that for the most part consist of relatively modest domiciles surrounded by a complex of out-buildings and animal pens. Glick (1979: 28-9) emphasized that most Visigoths were herders, in contrast to the Hispano-Romans who maintained a pattern of Mediterranean agriculture. This potentially testable distinction has not been followed up in the archaeological literature. The Visigoths were described as distinctive in the contemporary literature for their use of butter (or ghee) for cooking rather than olive oil (Bonnassie 1991b: 62). Recent advances in ceramic residue analysis might make it possible to distinguish archaeologically between the two cooking patterns.

For some time, the row-grave cemeteries and hamlet settlements of the Meseta have been regarded as signaling the arrival and settlement of Visigothic immigrants of a relatively lower social status, at least relative to upper nobility residing in cities or royal sites. Although this view has been vigorously criticized by some (e.g. Collins 2004: 174-86), in the final analysis it seems a perfectly reasonable argument. We need not assume that every single individual buried in these cemeteries was of Gothic heritage in order to accept that such sites are reflective of Visigothic presence, and it is quite likely that considerable intermarriage and enculturation occurred over time, as argued by Ripoll López.

Elite residences

The Visigoths had already formed a nascent state during their settlement in Aquitaine during the fifth century, so it is reasonable to assume that the group that moved into the Hispania was already strongly stratified. Heather notes that even by 376, Gothic society already consisted of permanent high status contingent called *optimates*, along with an entourage of followers and slaves (Heather 1992: 70). By the sixth century these permanent status roles had solidified into a hereditary nobility that mapped onto territorial organization in the form of the early medieval pattern of regional and local overlordship based upon regional military leaders referred to as dukes (*duces*), and lords of smaller districts or territories called counts (*comes*). We know from documentary evidence that many high ranking Gothic nobles lived in cities and towns (for the case of Mérida see Díaz 2000). Below these titled offices there undoubtedly existed a landed hereditary elite whose holdings were dispersed in the countryside. The dispersal of these lands, their holders and their tenant labourers would pose a problem for the Arab conquerors in the eighth century (see Chapters 1 and 3).

Archaeologically, the presence of these rural elites has not been particularly visible. Many of the large villas of the classical period were abandoned by the beginning of the fifth century, or were subsequently transformed into churches and/or cemeteries (Chavarría 2005; Chavarría & Lewit 2004; Ripoll López & Arce 2000). The site of Pla de Nadal (Navarro & Centelles Izquierdo 1986), located near Manises about 6 km west of Valencia, which Wickham describes as 'one of Europe's most impressive rural/secular buildings of the seventh/eighth centuries' (2005: 660), is almost certainly part of an elite residence dating to the late Visigothic period. The site of El Bovalar in Seròs (Lerida) about 90 km northwest of Tarragona is usually characterized as a 'rural settlement', although what kind of rural settlement is not clear. Excavations in the 1980s uncovered a basilica with three naves measuring 26 x 12 m in extent, with burials beneath the floor. Surrounding the ecclesiastical complex was an area about 2,000 m² filled with contiguous domiciles containing domestic refuse. This may be some kind of estate or perhaps a monastic settlement. The occupation layer is covered with a layer of ashes and charcoal, and just beneath the ash layer were found gold coins scattered in the debris that date to the last years of the Visigothic period. Two of the coins were minted in the name of a little known king named Achila, who apparently reigned very briefly after the demise of Rodrigo (Manzano Moreno 2006: 44), although Bonnassie (1991b) suggests that the Visigothic kingdom had at that point split into two, and Achila was actually reigning concurrently and for a few years after Rodrigo. In any case, it appears that the inhabitants of this locale put up some kind of resistance to the invasion, and the settlement was hastily abandoned, sacked and burned probably as the Arab conquerors moved into the Ebro valley in 714.

The Mediterranean littoral

The Mediterranean littoral is a key region for the comparative assessment of Visigothic vs. Roman contribution to the Late Roman pattern of settlement organization and material culture because it appears to have been relatively independent from Visigothic control for much of the period, and was in fact Byzantine territory for up to 75 years between 550 and around 620, as I will discuss in more detail below. Furthermore, while long-distance trade essentially ceased in most of the Peninsula, the littoral continues to carry on Mediterranean trade with ports in North Africa and the Levant into the early seventh century (Gutiérrez Lloret 1998a). With the fall of the last Byzantine stronghold, Carthago (Cartagena) in 621-2, the importation of ceramic wares, and the products they contained, ceases altogether.

Reynolds (2005) has provided a detailed summary of the pattern of imports and exports on the eastern and southern coast of Spain as reflected in amphorae and various classes of table and cooking wares. Basically, the Baetican export of olive oil, fish sauce and wine, which had been one of the main sources of wealth for Hispania, ceases after the fourth century when North Africa becomes the supplier of the *annona* for Rome. At this point, exports are limited to the shipment of oil further up the coast to Tarragona, Barcelona, Narbonne and Marseilles, and, to a limited extent, the movement of wine and fish sauce from Baetica and Lusitania up the Atlantic coast as far as Britain. After *c.* 500, exports, or at least the ones that leave interpretable archaeological traces, cease altogether. Imports to the eastern and southern littoral continue from two main sources: North Africa (particularly Algeria, Tunisia (Carthage) and the Tripolitanian coast) and the Levant. When

North Africa becomes the *annona* supplier to Rome, a portion of these products find their way to Hispania. Reynolds argues that the Vandal invasions of Carthage in the 430s disrupted the export of supplies from this region, and entrepreneurs from the Levant took advantage of the hiatus and began exporting goods to the Spanish coast. After export trade from Vandal-controlled North Africa was re-established in the 450s, the two main sources of long-distance trade to the littoral were the Levant and North Africa. Interestingly, one of the trade goods imported to the Spanish southeastern coast was hand-made cooking wares (Gutiérrez Lloret 1998a). Trade relations with the Algerian and Tunisian coast would continue until the beginning of the seventh century, after which Hispania becomes a 'self-sufficient world without imports' (Reynolds 2005: 440). In the ninth century, trade ties with both North Africa and the eastern Mediterranean are renewed, and form important sources of influence in the production of the new fine glazed wares that signal Islamization.

Vinalopó valley survey

The settlement survey of the Vinalopó valley carried out by Paul Reynolds (1993) in the early 1990s provides a picture of settlement reorganization and decline in the Late Roman period. The principal settlement in the region is Ilici (today Elche), a colony founded under Julius Caesar or Augustus which remained the central place of the region up to the end of the Visigothic period when it was a bishopric. During the fourth century, there was a decline in public building and in the size of cities and towns, along with a corresponding increase in the size and opulence of private residences (Keay 1988: 190-2). In the region of Ilici, many private villas were renovated and *garum* production sites along the coast continued to be used and rebuilt until the fourth century. During the first decades of the fifth century, however, the region underwent a major reorganization, during which the number of villas in the lowland areas near the mouths of rivers, including the

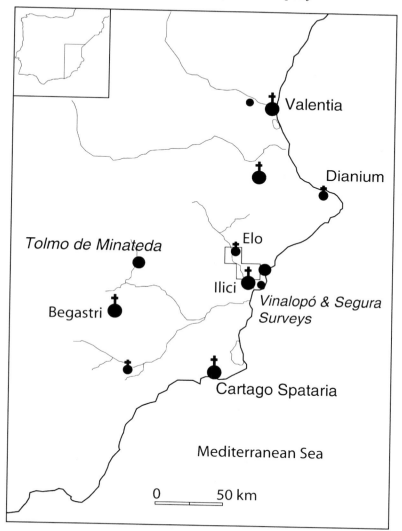

Fig. 2.5. Map of the Tudmir, showing the location of the known ecclesiastical seats and settlements, including Tolmo de Minateda, excavated by Abad Casal et al. (1998). Also shown are the locations of the Vinalopó (Reynolds 1993) and lower Segura river (Gutiérrez Lloret 1989) survey areas, discussed later in this chapter and in Chapter 3.

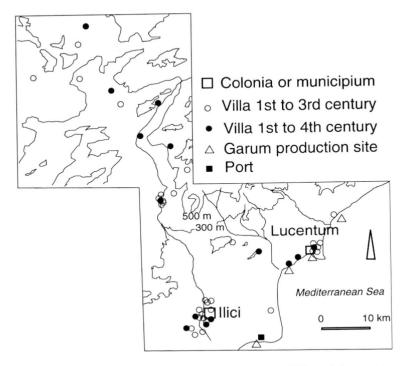

Fig. 2.6. Vinalopó Survey area, first to fourth century. This and the next two figures are intended to show the degree of settlement draw-down and movement to hilltop elevations from the fifth to the seventh century. Redrawn and simplified from Reynolds 1993: fig. 108.

Vinalopó, that flowed down from the mountains, began to decrease in number, and there is increased occupation, or in many cases reoccupation, of highland sites in the mountains further from the sea.

Reynolds interprets this shift to the highlands as primarily defensive, in the face of the increasing political instability that accompanied the evaporation of Roman control in the western Mediterranean in the early 400s. In fact, Reynolds suggests that the move to the highlands reflects a return to Bronze and early Iron Age settlement patterns. He further argues that

46

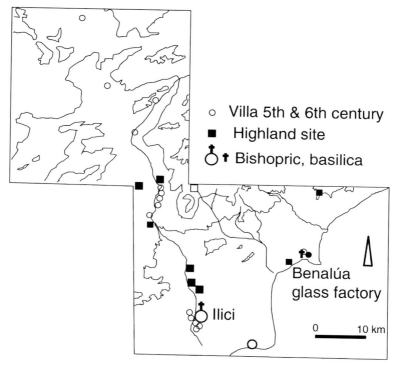

Fig. 2.7. Vinalopó Survey area, fifth and sixth centuries. Redrawn and simplified from Reynolds 1993: fig. 109.

these mountain sites may not have been self-sufficient, requiring the importation of foodstuffs from the coast. Hence the shift of imported fine wares from the lowland villas, which, though decreasing in number, remained self-sufficient, to the highlands, reflects this dependence on trade. However, it is not clear what the highland sites had to offer in return in order to procure these supplies.

After 450, virtually all the villas on the alluvial fan surrounding the bishopric of Ilici had been abandoned, although a few survived further up the Vinalopó valley around what would become the bishopric of Elo (El Monastil) during the Visigothic

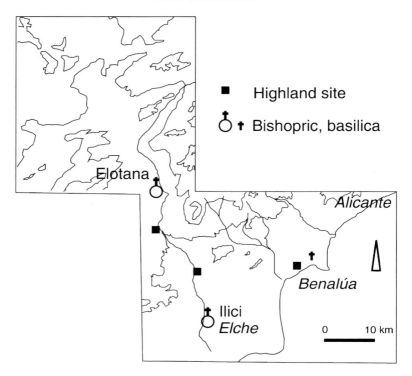

Fig. 2.8. Vinalopó Survey area, seventh century. Redrawn and simplified from Reynolds 1993: fig. 110.

period. The only coastal settlements that remain are the Late Roman and later Byzantine bishopric of Ilici and the Late Roman port settlement around La Albufereta and the hilltop settlement at Tossal de Manises, now both within present-day Alicante. A trash deposit associated with what appears to have been a glass factory has been excavated in the Barrio de Benalúa, on the southwest side of Alicante near the docks (1993: 14, 53). Glass bowls identical to those found as wasters at Benalúa have been recovered from other Visigothic period sites in the region, indicating the survival of some regional commerce during the sixth century.

2. The background of late antiquity

From 552 to the first decade of the 600s the region was incorporated into the Byzantine empire through the conquests of Justinian. There is very little in the archaeological record of the Vinalopó to reflect this eastern interlude beyond a few datable amphorae. This turbulent period in the history of the region is perhaps better reflected in the archaeology of the settlement of Tolmo de Minateda, discussed below.

Tolmo de Minateda

Tolmo de Minateda, located in the southeast corner of the province of Albacete about 85 km northwest of the city of Murcia near the town of Hellín, is a good example of a settlement that underwent a smooth transition from the late Roman to the Islamic period, thrived during the emiral period, then ran foul of the caliphate's centralizing tendencies and was destroyed or abandoned during the tenth century. The site is located on a limestone erosional remnant that forms an oblong mesa approximately 400 x 150 m overlooking the broad floodplain of the Arroyo de Tobarra, a permanent tributary of the rio Mundo and subsequently, the Segura, which empties into the Mediterranean just south of Alicante (Abad Casal et al. 1998).

The mesa top of Tolmo de Minateda is divided into to two main areas: El Regueron, which is tilted slightly and offers relatively easy access to the valley floor below by horseback or cart, and an upper platform which can be accessed only by a series of steps carved into the rock in antiquity. Both areas show evidence of occupation dating back to the Bronze Age, but it enters the historical period as the Roman *municipio* of Ilunum, located on the road from Carthago Nova (present-day Cartagena) to Complutum (Alcalá de Henares, near Madrid). The site had almost certainly been an important Iberian town before, as attested by the Iberian cemetery found at the foot of the mesa just to the north. So the settlement is not a new Roman foundation, but rather an indigenous settlement that became incorporated into the Roman system of colonias and municipios. A cut stone wall enclosing the Regueron, which bears an inscription in the name of Caesar Augustus, gives us a probable approximate date for the entrance of the town into the Roman orbit.

At the beginning of the fourth century, Diocletian created a new province out the region called Carthagensis, with Carthago Nova (Cartagena) as its capital. This would have created more traffic along the Complutum-Carthago Nova road, and a more vigorous market for agricultural producers in the area. In fact, there does seem to be archaeological evidence for increased population and economic activity in the *villae rusticae* of the surrounding area. Although olives are not a major crop in the area today, olive oil production may have been one of the main industries during the Roman and Byzantine periods – fixtures for grinding and pressing olives are found carved into the rock at Tolmo.

In 533, the Byzantine emperor Justinian launched a campaign of *renovatio imperii*, or restoration of the former empire. The Byzantine armies first took the Vandal kingdoms of North Africa, and then turned to the Italian Peninsula, which at the time was under the control of the Ostrogoths. Having regained Italy by 552, the Byzantine armies then turned to Spain, taking control of the southeastern coast of the Peninsula from the Guadalquivir river to the Júcar, just south of Valencia, including the coastal cities of Málaga and Cartagena. At this point, the settlement of Tolmo-*Ilunum* finds itself on the frontier between Visigothic lands in the central Peninsula and Byzantine holdings along the coast. In 589-90, the Byzantines began a campaign of strengthening the fortifications of Cartagena as well as of at least three other settlements within their Spanish holdings, including *Ilunum*. Excavations at Tolmo have in fact revealed evidence of a cut stone wall protecting the Reguerón, the most accessible part of the mesa top settlement, in many cases reusing materials from the wall built in the Augustan period nearly 600 years before. The construction style of the wall resembles that of the other Byzantine fortifications ordered by Justinian, suggesting that Tolmo was at the time occupied and fortified by the Byzantines. However, the Byzan-

2. The background of late antiquity

tines lost their hold on their Spanish possessions with their final defeat at Cartagena in 622, and the territories returned to the Visigoths. Tolmo almost certainly fell into Visigothic hands a couple of decades earlier. Ceramic and other artifacts found within the walls seem to point to a Visigothic occupation by the first half of the seventh century. Abad Casal, Gutiérrez Lloret and Sanz point out, however, that the construction of this fortification wall signals a major transformation in the morphology of the late Roman city, presaging the appearance of the medieval walled city (1998: 107).

At the end of the sixth century, following the conversion of the Visigothic king from Arianism to Roman Catholicism, new episcopal sees were created in the region at *Begastri* (now Cabezo de Roenas in Cehegín) and a settlement called *Elo* or *Eio*, which Abad Casal and Gutiérrez Lloret argue can be identified as the former imperial Roman settlement of *Ilunum*, now Tolmo de Minateda (confusingly, this see was moved in the later seventh century to the coastal settlement of *Ilici* – now Elche).

Aside from the toponymic similarities, the principal evidence for this interpretation is the discovery in the 1983-8 excavations of a substantial seventh-century basilica on the upper platform of the Tolmo, the excavation of which was completed in 2000-1 (Gutiérrez Lloret et al. 2004). The excavations and the outlines of the basilica are clearly visible on Google Earth satellite imagery. The basilica, with three naves supported by eighteen columns, measures about 37.5 x 12.5 m, including the baptistery, and its single apse adds another 6.2 m to its total length. Although there were no interments inside the building itself as in Mértola (see below), graves were distributed around the exterior of the building. This marks another transformation of the late Roman city, the movement of cemeteries from outside the city walls to the interior. Also in contrast with the Mértola basilica, none of the flat stones covering the sepultures bore epitaphs. All available evidence suggests that the structure was built at the end of the sixth century or the beginning of the seventh, remained in use right up until the Arab invasion, fell out of use sometime in the eighth century, and was in ruins by the ninth century, as a collection of houses from the emiral period were built on top of the ruins.

The southwest Iberian Peninsula: Mértola and its region

The last regional case study I will consider in this brief portrait of the diversity of late antique settlement history just prior to the Arab conquest is the region of Mértola in the Lower Alentejo of Portugal, in the southwest Iberian Peninsula. This is another area of the Peninsula that was under Byzantine influence, if not direct control, and following the retreat of Byzantine interests, there is little, if any, evidence of Visigothic presence in the region.

Mértola is a hilltop castle town located on a steep promontory perched between the confluence of the Ribeira Oeiras and the Guadiana river, which empties into the Atlantic Ocean some 70 km downriver (Lopes 2003). Located very near the highest navigable point on the river, Mértola was essentially a Mediterranean port from the Iron Age to medieval times. Products drawn the hinterland would have been collected at Mértola and loaded onto ships that went down the Guadiana and then east through the Strait of Gibraltar into the Mediterranean. The main products for which there is archaeological or documentary evidence are metals: mainly copper and iron, along with some lead, silver and gold. The region is located at the eastern end of the Pyrite Belt that includes, just across the border with Spain to the east, the famous Rio Tinto mines. Wool and hides are another likely product for export; from the sixteenth to the early twentieth centuries Mértola was on the southern end of a 270 km sheep-herding transhumance route that connected the Lower Alentejo with the Serra de Estrela in central Portugal. A traditional blanket-weaving industry in Mértola produces blankets with design motifs that can be found on Islamic period pottery found in excavation in the Alcaçaba (Torres 1984).

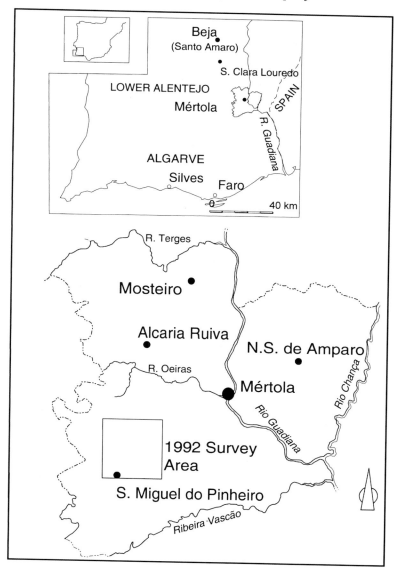

Fig. 2.9. Map of Mértola and its surrounding region.

With the exception of an interlude in the early fifth century involving the Suevi, and possibly the Vandals and Alans, this area seems to remain dominated politically and culturally by Hispano-Romans right up to the Arab Conquest. Hydatius mentions that Mértola was successfully besieged by the Suevi under Rechila in 440 (Thompson 1982: 171). In the district capital of Beja (Roman *Pax Julia*), there is a fifth- and sixth-century basilica, Santo Amaro, that has now been converted into an archaeological museum called the Núcleo Visigótico, which is something of a misnomer. An excavation during the 1950s in what had been an extramural cemetery next to the structure yielded a burial of an adult male with a sword with a hilt decorated with garnet cloisonné work, as well as two fibulae, also decorated with garnet stones and inlay. Kouznetsov and Lebedynsky (2005: 120) have tied this sword hilt stylistically to the Caucasus region in the early fifth century, and suggest that this burial represents an Alan who arrived with the Vandal/Alanic invasion of the first decade of the fifth century.

Some of the large Roman villas in the region, such as three located near Beja: Pisões, Santa Clara de Louredo (see below; Gorges 1979), Monte Cigonha (Lopes & Alfenim 1994) and Villa Moura, also called Cerro da Vila near Loulé, in the Algarve (Matos 1994) show continuity of settlement well into the late Roman period and in some cases (Monte Cigonha and Villa Moura) on into the Islamic period. A funerary stone found at the site of Vale de Aguilhão in the village of Santa Clara de Louredo located about halfway between Mértola and Beja carries a moving inscription written in the first person by a Hispano-Roman named Calandronius, mourning the death of his fifteen-year-old niece, Maura, dated 29 July 665 (Correia & Oliveira 1993: 79). The inscription is written in block capitals on marble from outside the area rather than in cursive on local slate, as in the *pizarras* of the Spanish Meseta. Little is actually known about the site (it is catalogued in Gorges 1979), but it is apparently a villa dating back at least to the third century, which is apparently still occupied by a literate Hispano-Roman elite towards the end of the seventh century.

2. The background of late antiquity

The Paleochristian basilica at Mértola, located beneath a modern plaza, the Rossio de Carmo and an adjoining primary school, was excavated in 1981-9 by a team from Campo Arqueológico de Mértola (Lopes 2003: 144-56; Torres & Macías 1993) provide further evidence for a continuing Hispano-Roman landed elite in the region of Mértola. Located beneath a modern plaza, the Rossio de Carmo and an adjoining primary school, the structure was excavated in 1981-3 by a team from Campo Arqueológico de Mértola, an archaeological research group based in Mértola with whom I have collaborated since 1987. Excavations at the basilica revealed over 50 grave stones with epitaphs which reflect a continuing, but declining population from the fifth century to the beginning of the eighth. The earliest group of interments is from beneath the floor of the basilica itself and from an area beneath a contemporary plaza surface just outside the building. These are clearly associated with the use of the basilica as a place of burial during the fifth to seventh centuries.

Most of the tombs, which were often in the form of stone and plaster lined cysts carved into the underlying bedrock, were covered with flat stone covers, 52 of which had legible inscriptions giving information regarding the names, ages at death, dates of death, and in some cases the occupation or social class of the interred. These epitaphs record the burial of members of Hispano-Roman elite families (*honestiores*), religious devotees (presbyters, monks and nuns), who were themselves often drawn from such families. One epitaph in Greek records a foreigner named Eutekius, who was born in Libya and died in Mértola in 544.

There are other lines of material evidence that reflect strong ties with North Africa and the eastern Mediterranean (Macías 1993). The plan of the basilica itself is a double apse form that has parallels in Proconsular Africa (Tunisia) during the same period. A fibula recovered from one burial has been identified as Byzantine style (Lopes 2003: 151-2). Ceramic pieces found with burials include a Hayes form 92 *terra sigillata* bowl manufactured in Phocaea. At least five of the tombstones have carved representations of a horseshoe arch, an architectural form originating in Syria (see Chapter 5) usually supported by twisted cord columns with Corinthian capitals.

Some of the prepared tombs contained more than one burial, evidence that the tombs were reused, perhaps to inter additional family members. Of the 40 grave stones which carried dates of death, 6 (15%) were from the late fifth century, 24 (60%) from the first half of the sixth century (500-50), 7 (17.5%) were from 550-600, 2 were from 601-700, and a single stone was dated 706, five years before the Muslim invasion.

The basilica apparently fell out of use or collapsed or was torn down at some point following the Muslim invasion in 711. Since the region is tectonically active, it is possible an earthquake destroyed the building. Aside from the well-known earthquake of 1755 that affected the area, an earthquake in 1550 collapsed the roof of the mosque-church located outside the walls of the *al-caçova* and occasioned its complete renovation.

A second group of interments was excavated from the rubble mound above the building itself and are of a markedly different character. The basilica inhumations were all in supine position with heads oriented west-northwest, following the orientation of the structure and the direction of sunset. In contrast, bodies recovered from the rubble layer overlaying the basilica were all positioned lying on their sides and slightly flexed, heads oriented south and facing the east, the direction of Mecca. No recognizable gravestones were associated with these burials, nor was there any special preparation of the graves themselves. The positioning of these burials is consistent with Islamic period burials found elsewhere in the region, and differs markedly from that of fourteenth- and fifteenth-century medieval Christian burials recovered from a nearby cemetery located in the Alcaçova de Mértola, which were again supine and oriented towards the west.

At least three other Late Roman religious sites are known in the surrounding *concelho* of Mértola (Lopes 2003: 160-4). These include the parish churches of Nossa Senhora de Amparo and São Bartolomeu de Via Gloria, as well as the now-defunct church and monastery of São Salvador in the village of Mosteiro. Carved stones incorporated into the present-day chapel at São Bartolomeu indicate that a Paleochristian religious structure existed on that site in the late Roman period. A small occupation site adjacent to the chapel contains late *terra sigillata* or red-slipped sherds, as well as roof tiles with zigzag designs and thumb-impressions, indicative of the late Roman period (the zigzag style continues on into the Islamic period). Similar tiles have been found in a buried occupation layer exposed by a road-cut adjacent to the present-day hilltop chapel of Nossa Senhora de Amparo, where late Roman/Visigothic-style carved stone was also found during a recent renovation of the church. Hence, São Bartolomeu and Nossa Senhora de Amparo were religious sites in the late Roman period and were again used as the sites of parish churches with the formation of the parochial system in the area in the fifteenth and sixteenth centuries. There is no indication of their continued use as religious structures during the 500-year Islamic period itself, suggesting either a remarkable locational coincidence or an equally remarkable continuity of cultural memory present in the area during the medieval Islamic period.

Ermida de São Salvador is a late Roman period church that was associated with a monastic community (Lopes 2003: 162). This partially standing building and associated site is located in the modern village of Mosteiro, about 20 km northwest of Mértola. The old building has been incorporated into a modern house and barn compound. Fragments of marble columns and Roman tegulae can be seen incorporated into the dry stone masonry walls of the more recent construction, and this is probably an example of a Roman villa that became a church and monastery in the later Roman period. The inhabitants of the village are well aware that the building was once a church. A white cross, fashioned out of quartz cobbles, can be seen built into the wall of the adjoining house. Subsequent research has revealed that the building probably has not been used as a church since the seventh or eighth century. It was not mentioned in the inventory of churches made by Portuguese officials in 1482 and 1565. The only mention of the church that has been found was in an inventory collated by a Benedictine order in 1644 (*Obra Beneditina Lusitana*), which indicates that it had been a church called São Salvador before the 'coming of the Moors', and had been associated with a Benedictine monastery. Justino Maciel has suggested that the community may have served as a *xenodochium*, or way-house for travellers and pilgrims. A series of burials with stone slab coverings have recently been excavated, and are clearly associated with the use of the building as a church. Roman tegulae have been found in the vicinity of this site and a nearby hilltop.

A settlement survey carried out by myself in an 8 x 8 km² quadrat 24 km west of Mértola has provided new information on secular rural settlement in the Late Roman and Islamic period in the area (Boone & Worman 2007). Roman settlement begins in the early first century BC with the establishment of what Alarcão (1988: 109-10) has called fortified villas, and continues into the fourth and fifth centuries with small farmsteads and one or two modest villas. With the withdrawal of Roman military protection in the first decade or two of the fifth century, the small villas and Roman farmsteads in the survey area were abandoned and never reoccupied. Although central places like Mértola and a few religious sites (discussed above) are known to have continued, there is a period of rural site archaeological invisibility that lasts for perhaps two centuries until the late sixth or seventh century.

Sixteen habitation sites from the very late Roman and early Islamic period were identified. I have termed these sites 'transitional' because they lack material that is distinctive of either the earlier Roman period or the succeeding later Islamic period, although most of them probably date to the emiral period. One of these sites, Queimada, is radiocarbon-dated securely in the late sixth and seventh centuries; two other sites that have been excavated date from the late seventh to mid-tenth centuries (Boone & Worman 2007: Table 1). Roman tegulae-style roof tiles are absent in these sites, and roofs were constructed using

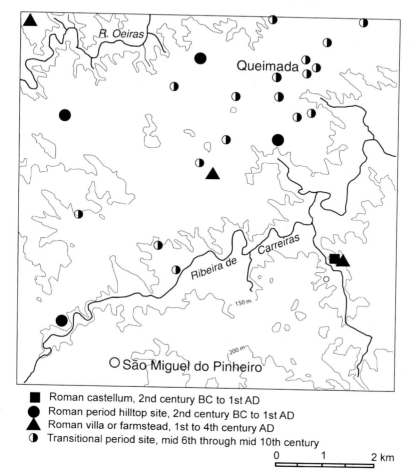

Fig. 2.10. Map of survey area near Mértola (simplified from Boone and Worman 2007), showing the location of Roman, late Roman, and transitional period (mid-sixth to mid-tenth century) sites.

only the tapered half-cylindrical *imbrex* tiles. Unlike Europe north of the Pyrenees and in Italy in the Dark Ages (Ward-Perkins 2005: 79, 109), roof tiles continue to be manufactured and used, even in humble rural structures. These sites repre-

59

sent hamlets consisting of only one or two tile-roofed house structures built of dry-stone masonry. Pottery consisted of hand-formed cooking and water storage wares produced from local clays, with increasing frequencies of wheel-thrown pottery in the later part of the period. This could be the result of a shift to a higher volume pottery industry stimulated by an increase in the number of consumers, whereby wheel-made production offers increasing economy of scale. Alternatively, the shift to wheel production might signal the reintroduction of a wheel industry by Muslim potters. The same pattern of pottery production and distribution is found on the eastern coast of Spain during the same period, and I will discuss this pattern in more detail in Chapter 5.

These small hamlets and villages began to appear in the region perhaps fifty to a hundred years before the Muslim invasion of 711, and they continued with no radical break in material culture, other than a gradual increase in the frequency of wheel-thrown common wares, until about 950-1000, when rural settlements start to aggregate and move to hilltop locations, and glazed Islamic table wares and lamps start to appear in small quantities (see further discussion in Chapter 5).

Conclusions

The three focal areas discussed above generally support Ripoll López and Velázquez's contention, cited at the beginning of this chapter, that historical development in Hispania in the late Roman period resembles that of the rest of Europe and the Mediterranean. Visigothic burial and secular and ecclesiastical settlement broadly resembles that of the Franks north of the Pyrenees, while the Mediterranean littoral and southwest corner of the Peninsula show strong parallels with the North African coast, particularly Tunisia and Libya, and the eastern Mediterranean.

Based on the material evidence, the Visigoths seem to be a case of an ethnic elite that was more or less completely assimilated into late Roman culture and society. Although the documentary evidence, mainly in the form of laws and legislation, offers an important window on the paper-poor seventh century, it may be that these documents give an exaggerated view of Visigothic presence on the landscape. Archaeologically, aside from the coins and a few hundred known burials, the Visigoths would be nearly invisible. In this world, Roman culture, the culture of the indigenous people, was the prestige culture, rather than that of the Gothic invaders and immigrants. Hence the direction of enculturation went from indigenous to newcomers. We will see that in the case of the Arab conquest, this direction is completely reversed.

The idea that the Visigothic Spain was on a downward spiral of decline at the time of the Arab conquest in 711 is a recurring theme in the historiography of the period. For some, it provides an explanation why the Arabs were able to subdue the Peninsula so rapidly and decisively. For others, the Arab conquest constitutes a kind of poetic justice, sweeping away the corrupt, low-ceilinged world of the northern barbarians and replacing it with a cosmopolitan, communitarian, urbane culture of the East. The seventh century certainly does mark a demographic, economic and cultural low-point in the first millennium, but the fact is that this is just as true for the rest of Europe and the western Mediterranean (Ward-Perkins 2005). Nor are the causes of the decline in Hispania entirely endogenous to Visigothic society. This was a colder (Larsen 2008), and possibly drier period between the Roman and medieval Optima (Koder 1996). Frequent droughts and locust plagues are a feature of the this period, although they continue into the eighth century after the Arab conquest (Glick 1979: 29, 32). Furthermore, although plague has long been known to be a recurrent feature of the the sixth to eighth centuries, Lester K. Little and others (Little 2007) have recently re-emphasized what a formative effect this pandemic had on late Roman society around the Mediterranean starting in 541 and lasting until 750. Specifically, the pandemic appears to have derailed Justinian's attempt to regain the western empire in Hispania, and its recurrence every couple of generations must have impeded demographic recovery, although its effects on the interior of the Peninsula are difficult to assess (Kulikowski 2007).

During the last decades of Visigothic rule there is documentary evidence, in the form of laws designed to enforce the regular convening of troops, that the kings were having difficulty rounding up an army in times of conflict (Manzano Moreno 2006: 33). Individuals who failed to respond to calls to arms by the king were threatened with the penalty of confiscation of property. Manzano Moreno argues that Visigothic aristocrats were reticent to send their entourages and dependants off on military campaigns from which they might never return. This in turn suggests a spiralling discrepancy between the political and economic interests of the landed nobility and the monarchy itself, exacerbated by the increasing centralizing tendencies of the monarchy as reflected in the draconian laws enacted against Jews, heretics and escaped slaves that appear in the closing decades. These are policies that would return with a vengeance (and adding moriscos to the list of the persecuted) on the eve of Castile's rise to world power in the sixteenth century. The alienation of the aristocracy meant that at the time of the Arab invasion, different regions and territories in Iberia were left to their own devices. Each region, under the local rule of Visigothic or Hispano-Roman counts or bishops, was left to make its own deal with the Arabs, and none on its own could put up an effective defense. The only major battle in which the Arab and Berber armies engaged Visigothic forces *per se* was the first one, with Roderigo.

3

The formation of al-Andalus

In 711, Musa ibn Nusayr, governor of the newly conquered North African province of the Arab empire, sent a force of between seven and twelve thousand Berber soldiers led by his Berber client, or *mawla*, Tariq ibn Ziyad, across the Strait of Gibraltar into the Iberian Peninsula. Near the present-day town of Medina Sidonia, they met with Christian forces under the leadership of the Visigothic king, Roderigo, and in the ensuing battle, defeated them. Tariq was joined within the year by a second army led by Musa himself, which marched to Toledo, the capital of the Visigothic kingdom, and forced its surrender. Over the next five years, the two forces of Tariq and Musa, along with a third army led by Musa's son Abdul Azziz, captured most of the important cities of the Iberian Peninsula.

The subsequent 750-year Islamic occupation of the Iberian Peninsula can be divided into several phases, based principally on changing patterns of sociopolitical control (the brief summary below is drawn from Kennedy 1996, which is the best source in English; see also Manzano Moreno 2006). A period of settling in extends from about 715, when a governor of the conquered territory was appointed, to the foundation of an independent emirate in 756. The Arab conquest of North Africa and the Iberian Peninsula had been directed by a centralized Islamic state centred on Damascus, under the control of the Umayyad dynasty. In 750, just forty years after the initial invasion of the Iberian Peninsula, the Umayyad dynasty in Damascus fell to a competing family, the Abbasids, who then moved the capital to Baghdad. When the Abbasids came to power, they attempted to exterminate every member of the

Umayyad dynasty who might rise back up and claim legitimacy to rule. However, a few survivors took refuge in the Maghreb and the Iberian Peninsula. Abd al-Rahman ibn Mu'awiya, the son of a North African Berber woman of the Nafza tribe who was a slave in the court of Damascus, became the first emir of al-Andalus in 756 and nominally declared independence of the Andalusian state from Damascus.

Abd al-Rahman's arrival in al-Andalus came at a time when competing factions of the tribal armies, the Northern (Qaysi) and Southern (Yemeni) Arabs, as well as dissatisfied Berber tribes in hinterlands, were immersed in protracted internecine warfare. The emiral period, from 756 to 929, marks a time of fitful economic and urban growth around which a more sophisticated and centralized political system centred on Córdoba ultimately crystallized. Although the critical transition period was the reign of Abd al-Rahman II (822-52), a period of decline and disorder lasting over fifty years followed, and the Córdoban state was not proclaimed a caliphate until 929, under Abd al-Rahman III. The unified Córdoban caliphate, under which a brilliant Andalusian civilization flourished, was to last barely a hundred years. Power struggles among various factions involving Berbers, the original landed Arab aristocracy and the central state, effectively suppressed during the reign of Abd al-Rahman III, surfaced again in the late caliphate and erupted into civil war in 1009-10 (Scales 1994). One of the principal victims of the insurrection was the city of Córdoba itself, which was sacked and burned.

The outcome was the political fragmentation of al-Andalus into as many as fifteen petty kingdoms called *taifas* beginning around 1031 (Wasserstein 1985). The *taifa* leaders abandoned any pretence of regaining the caliphate, and called themselves by lesser titles, creating serious legitimacy problems, while at the same time attempting to maintain the form of caliphal opulence and conspicuous expenditure in their relations with each other. These expenditures, along with the severely reduced tax base they had to draw from, forced the *taifa* leaders to increase their tax demands on the primary producers under

3. The formation of al-Andalus

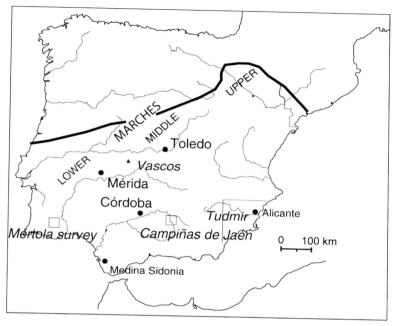

Fig. 3.1. Map of the Iberian Peninsula in the Islamic period, showing the location of cities, places and sites discussed in the text.

their jurisdiction, mainly in form of uncanonical taxes. The *taifas* along the frontier had difficulty defending themselves against the expanding Christian kingdoms to the north and were forced to enter into costly tribute relationships with them, a prelude to outright conquest. After Toledo fell to the Christians in 1086, the North African Almoravid state was invited to bring in its armies to assist in the defence of the Muslim kingdoms. The Almoravids took advantage of their military presence to seize control and proclaim al-Andalus a province of their North African empire, centred on Marrakesh. The North African Berber dynasties would rule al-Andalus through the Almoravid period (1086-1147) and the subsequent Almohad period (1147-1248), but they themselves were unstable, locked in a cycle of rapid rise and expansion followed by abrupt decline and contraction, vividly described by Ibn Khaldun. Throughout this time, the Christian kingdoms made steady advances into Muslim territories. By the time of the breakup of the Almohad dynasty in the mid-twelfth century, only the kingdom of Granada, in the southeast corner of the Peninsula, remained in Muslim control. Protected by a ring of mountains and its proximity by direct sea route to North Africa, Granada, under a local dynasty known as the Nasrids, held on until 1492. A substantial Muslim population remained in Iberia under Christian rule until 1607, when the Spanish monarchy forced their conversion and expulsion (Butzer et al. 1986; Catlos 2004).

The bilingual dinars

One of the most remarkable archaeological 'footprints' of the beginning of the new order comes in the form of the gold coins that were struck within a year following the arrival of the conquerors in the spring of 711 (Manzano Moreno 2006: 55-63). These coins are known only from archaeological finds; there is no mention of them in the documentary evidence. Weighing a little over four grams, the coins are modelled after the Byzantine *solidus* of the same weight – in fact the earliest examples bear the Latin legend '*Hic solidus feritus in Spania annus XCIIII*' (This solidus was minted in Hispania in the year 94, i.e. of the Hegira, or AD 712). Later examples are called *solidus* in Latin on one side and *dinar* in Arabic on the other. The bilingual examples bear the first known reference to 'al-Andalus' by name.

Manzano Moreno points out that the first issue in 712 coincides with the arrival of Musa ibn Nusayr in the Peninsula with a new army, to join Tariq's newly successful forces. These coins stylistically resemble coins minted in North Africa under Musa's governorship, and are distinct from the dinars minted since 697 in the rest of the empire. Hence, before he had even completed the conquest of the Peninsula, Musa was already minting dinars, clearly expressing his intention to establish a government in the new territory. The coins were minted for two more years until Musa was called back to Damascus by the Umayyad caliph, who had become suspicious of Musa's aspirations. Musa left his two sons in charge as governors of al-Andalus, further suggesting that he had dynastic pretensions, but one son, Abd al-Aziz, was assassinated in Seville in about 715, and the new caliph moved his brother, Abd Allah, to the governorship of Ifriqiya. The gold dinars disappear from the record for two years. In 716, a new governor, unrelated to Musa, is appointed to al-Andalus, and the dinars again are minted, this time in their bilingual form, with the first reference to al-Andalus, but for only a year or two. When gold dinars minted in al-Andalus reappear again in 721, they are entirely in Arabic, and are stylistically identical to the dinars minted in the rest of the Arab empire. Gold dinars continued to be sporadically minted in al-Andalus until about 745, a period of turbulence caused by Berber revolts and by the introduction of the Arab *junds*, and gold dinars would not be minted in al-Andalus again until the establishment of the caliphate in 929.

The pattern of Arab conquest and settlement

The Arab conquest and settlement of Iberia differed from that of other areas of Arab expansion, in that the armies were not settled in specially designated garrison towns as they were in Iraq (Kufa), Egypt (Cairo), and Tunisia (Kairouan). In the early stages of the conquest of al-Andalus, the Arabs established fortifications called *qala/*s along important communications routes between existing cities, but they did not grow into large capital cities as they did in Iraq, Egypt or Tunisia. The locations of these forts are sometimes preserved in modern place names, such as Calatrava, located on the route between Córdoba and Toledo, or Alcalá de Henares, on the road between Toledo and Zaragoza. Instead, the relative lack of central control over the conquerors seems to have led to a situation in which the Arab invaders and their mainly Berber clients became themselves conquering elites, taking direct control of the lands they appropriated, and becoming landowners themselves. They were referred to as *baladiyyun* (from the Arabic word *balad*, land). This early development would have lasting implications for the way the power of central state unfolded in later centuries, as I will discuss in more detail in the next chapter.

Traditionally, Arab and Berber conquerors and settlers were held to have settled al-Andalus according to a simple formula: the Arabs took possession of the more valuable irrigable lands around the mouths and estuaries of major rivers and in the karstic spring fed valleys in the mountains of southeast Andalusia, while the Berbers had to settle for the dry farming regions of the central part of the Peninsula. While this appears to be the case as a general rule, there are important exceptions. For example, Guichard (1969; 1998) has shown that Valencia, located at the mouth of the Turia river and the centre of a major irrigated region along the coast, was first settled by Berbers. In contrast, the provincial capital of Beja (Portugal), which has rich volcanic soils but no irrigation, was settled by one of the Arab *junds* in the mid-eighth century. An updated view of the pattern of Arab and Berber settlement puts the majority of Arab settlement in two key areas: the Ebro valley in the former Tarraconensis and the Guadalquivir valley in the former Baetica, along with a smaller area of settlement in the karstic limestone regions of southeastern Andalusia where spring-fed irrigation was possible.

In Acién Almansa's (1999) formulation, early Arab settlement proceeded in two waves: first the installation of Arab governors in the old episcopal seats located in what had been Roman cities; second, some thirty years later, the settlement of the Syrian *junds* around half a dozen key areas of the southern Peninsula. The *junds* were groups of soldiers who were clients of the Umayyad dynasty in Damascus, which formed organizational units within the Arab military, deriving identity from the geographic location where they were originally stationed in Syria. In 739, a Berber rebellion against the Arab conquerors erupted in North Africa and the Umayyad caliph in Damascus sent an army from Syria to suppress the rebellion, but they were defeated and were forced to take refuge in Ceuta, a tiny

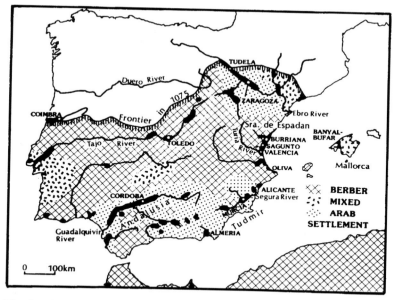

Fig. 3.2. Map showing areas of Arab and Berber settlement, and areas of irrigation vs. dry farming (Butzer et al.1985: fig. 1).

stronghold jutting off the northern peninsula of Morocco, just across the Strait of Gibraltar from Spain. The leader of the *junds* struck a deal with the governor of al-Andalus whereby they were put in charge of collecting taxes from the Christians who lived in each district, and would receive one third of the taxes they collected. The remaining two-thirds would go to the central state (Manzano Moreno 1998: 88-9). There were six *jund* units, who eventually settled in Elvira (Granada), Seville, Niebla, the vicinity of Ronda, Jaén, Algeciras, Medina Sidonia, Beja, and the district of Tudmir, in present-day Murcía and Alicante (see discussion below).

Given the far-flung nature of *jund* settlement, and the limited resources of the central government, the local power of the *junds* understandably began to increase. One can easily imagine that the *junds* might establish estates of their own in the localities where they became tax collectors, coming in time to resemble feudal lords, even though in theory they did not necessarily own the lands worked by the peasants they collected taxes from. In fact, suppression of the power of the *junds* becomes a central preoccupation of the first emir, Abd al-Rahman I (ruled 756-88) who eventually broke the *junds'* control over the hinterlands by playing one faction against another, and by recruiting Berber and slave contingents, who had no previous ties of clientage to competing factions, into the government.

The system (as well as the circumstances) under which the junds were settled in al-Andalus bears a striking resemblance to the way Goffart (1980) suggests the barbarians were settled into the former Roman provinces, and Manzano Moreno (1998: 90) argues that this system is quite similar to a system of *autopragia* imposed by the Visigothic monarchy (a system in which great landowners or towns collect the taxes on their lands themselves, keeping part for themselves as payment, and passing the rest on the state or monarch), although the details regarding how, or even whether, taxes were collected during this period are obscure. This similarity has sometimes been used as evidence for historical continuity between Visigothic and Arab rule, and an argument for assimilation of the Arabs into Hispanic culture. The similarity, however, results from the fact that both systems had common origins in late Roman imperial tax collection systems – in the case of the early Arab system, it derived from Byzantine practice. I will return to this issue several times in succeeding chapters.

Archaeological perspectives on early Islamic settlement in al-Andalus

Several regional studies have used documentary and archaeological evidence to trace the theme of 'the formation of Andalus', that is, the transformation of late Roman society and culture to an Islamic under emiral and caliphal rule. Prominent examples include the work of Azuar Ruiz (1989) on the Denía Peninsula just south of Valencia, Martínez Enamorado

(2003) on Rayya and Takurunna in the region between Ronda and Málaga, Salvatierra Cuenca (Salvatierra Cuenca 1993; 1997; Salvatierra Cuenca & Castillo Armenteros 1991; Salvatierra Cuenca et al. 1998) on Jaén, and Gutiérrez Lloret (1996) on the *kura* of Tudmir in Alicante and Murcia. Considerations of space prevent a detailed description of each of these in turn, and I will focus on Gutiérrez Lloret's foundational work on Tudmir, which was also discussed in Chapter 2.

From the late 1980s through the mid-1990s, Sonia Gutiérrez Lloret carried out an extensive regional study of the ancient *kura* of Tudmir, which encompasses the present-day provinces of Murcia, Alicante and a small corner of Albacete along the southeast coast of Spain (Gutiérrez Lloret 1996; 1998b; refer back to Fig. 2.5 on p. 45). This region had been the dependency, a kind of county called a *vicarius*, of the Visigothic count Theodemir at the time of the conquest. Theodemir then made a treaty with Abd al-Aziz ibn Musa in 712, which promised that he would remain on office as governor of his lands as well as freedom and security to the populus in return for a *per capita* tax of 1 dinar (a gold coin typically weighing a little over four grams, or an equivalent weight of gold), four *almudes* each of wheat and barley, four measures each of vinegar, unfermented grape juice or syrup, honey and olive oil (Barceló 1997b: 28; Reynolds 1993: 28). This was halved for slaves or serfs.

Theodemir died by 743 and the office went to his son Athanagild. But in 746 Athanagild was punished for some infraction and forced to pay a fine of 27,000 dinars, and the administration of his lands was transferred to the charge of the Syrian *jund* that had been recently stationed there, presumably under the terms discussed in the above section. In the same year, one of Theodemir's daughters married into the family of the Banu Hattab, an aristocratic Arab family settled in Murcia, and Theodemir and his family pass out of history save for the name, Tudmir, given to the newly formed *kura* (an administrative district in emiral and caliphal al-Andalus) based on his former Visigothic *vicarius*.

The *kura* of Tudmir encompassed at least seven towns, located

71

at or near the present-day towns of Orihuela, Elche and Alicante in the province of Alicante; Lorca, Mula and *Begastri* (the present-day site of Cabezo Roenas) in Murcia; and Hellín (actually Tolmo de Minateda) in Albacete (see a full discussion of the identification of these in Gutiérrez Lloret 1997: 222-74). Her archaeological investigations at Tolmo de Minateda offer a detailed example of what happens to late Roman urban settlement under emiral and caliphal rule. The Visigothic/late Roman settlement of *Ilunum/Elo/Eio* becomes the Islamic city of *Madinat Iyih* (later altered to its present-day name, Minateda).

The fortifications built by the Byzantines protecting the Reguerón, or lower part of the settlement, appear to have been in a state of disrepair and partial collapse at the time of the conquest. At some point early in the emiral period, new fortification walls of earth and stone were hastily built to protect this area, destroying a series of habitations from the Visigothic period. New houses were built behind the wall, but were subsequently abandoned, and the main part of the Islamic period settlement moved to the upper platform. On the upper platform, domestic structures cover the area around the old basilica. Inside the basilica itself, now collapsed or torn down, a series of pottery kilns were built. The new houses, however, are built of the same materials and organized spatially in the same way as the previous Visigothic period habitations, suggesting a considerable amount of continuity between the two periods. 'Islamization' at the household level, as would be reflected in household spatial organization and ceramic assemblages (discussed in Chaper 5 and in the discussion below of Pechina), does not occur until at least a century later in this region.

Three documentary sources of the period state that Madinat Iyih was ordered to be destroyed in 835 by the emir Abd al-Rahman II, during a series of struggles with local Arab factions, the descendants of the Arab *junds*, who were attempting to maintain autonomy from the central state in Córdoba. As in a similar case in the *kura* of Jaén, the emir founded a completely new urban settlement to break the power of the existing local aristocracy, in this case the city of *Madina Mur-siyya*, or present-day Murcia.

Cities in al-Andalus

Manzano Moreno (2006: 240-1) has suggested that a major shift in the focus and movement of population and economic activity took place between the late Roman and Islamic periods. In classical and late antique times Hispania was organized principally along two main axes: one, a north-south line that connected Seville (Hispalis), Mérida (Emerita) and León (Leges) along the Old Silver Road up to Asturias, and the other along the Levantine Coast, connecting the Mediterranean coastal ports of Málaga, Cartagena, Tarragona and Barcelona by water, and by land along the Via Augusta. It was along these two axes that populations of foreign traders from Syria, Asia Minor and Libya were concentrated, based on the occurrence of tombstone epitaphs bearing eastern Mediterranean names (Ripoll López 1998), and which presumably was the route by which Eastern artistic and symbolic influences, discussed in Chapter 5, came into Hispania in late antiquity. After the Arab conquest, the principal economic axis had shifted to the Guadalquivir valley – Seville and especially Córdoba – northeast to the Ebro valley by way of Toledo and Zaragoza.

Traditional views held that the city had nearly ceased to exist in Late Roman Iberia with decline setting in by the end of the third century. More recent archaeological work has shown that this view is too extreme – Roman-founded cities continued to thrive and evolve, but in a different form (Gutiérrez Lloret 1998b; Kennedy 1998). Whereas imperial Roman cities in the provinces had functioned principally as centres for the collection of land tax, late Roman cities become cultic centres focused on churches or basilicas, with many of the functions of patronage shifting from the state to the church. The main changes to the structure of cities during this period were the abandonment of public architecture and of public works such as centralized sewer systems, the movement of cemeteries from outside the city to its interior, typically in or around basilicas and churches, and the addition of city walls and fortifications. New construction was typically undertaken using materials from earlier public works, necessitating the razing or destruction of classical period construction, and giving a heightened appearance of decline and deterioration.

Islamic cities are one aspect of the material record that represents a sharp break with late Roman tradition, at least in theory. Quite a few important cities of al-Andalus developed out of pre-existing urban foundations, nearly all of them episcopal sees, and their succeeding development and morphology was constrained in this way to varying degrees. Public works including extensive aqueducts and sewer systems are reintroduced; the public bath makes a comeback after three or four centuries of absence – all urban features that the Arabs had inherited from the Byzantines. Large public plazas with a conspicuous display of statuary and public monuments are gone, although the latter had disappeared from the late Roman city as well. Souks become the principal public space in Islamic cities. Mosques replace basilicas and churches, with much of their splendour limited to interior space. About the only major urban feature that cities in the the two periods have in common are city walls.

A good example of the development of an Islamic city out of a previously existing Roman centre is Córdoba itself, the capital of al-Andalus. Late Roman *Corduba* consisted of a relatively small, compact walled urban nucleus containing the principal basilica, a government palace complex, and the domiciles of the city's service personnel, surrounded by numerous outlying village settlements called *vici* (sing. *vicus*) and palace villas where important government officials and aristocrats lived. Corduba was traditionally thought to have gone into to decline already by the end of the third century, but excavations during the 1990s along the northwest margins of the city that revealed a large and opulent palace complex outside the walls, referred to as *Cercadilla*, altered this view (Acién Almansa & Vallejo Triano 1998). However, during the fifth and especially the sixth

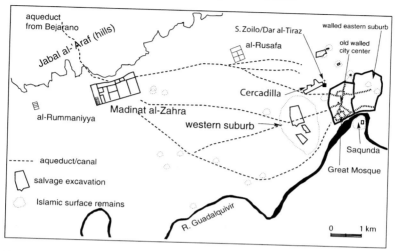

Fig. 3.3. Map of Córdoba in the Caliphal period. Based on Nicolle (2003) and Acién Almansa and Vallejo (1998).

centuries, there was clearly depopulation of the old centre of the city and a shift in occupation to the south of the city along the margins of the river. Here were constructed a new palace of the governor and the basilica of San Vicente, which would become the site of the Great Mosque. This shift in urban settlement seems to be connected with Byzantine control of the city during the second half of the sixth century. By the time Córdoba was successfully besieged by Arab forces in 712, the city nucleus was plainly in decline. The capital of the region had moved to Seville, the old Roman bridge across the Guadalquivir (a well-known landmark still standing today) was impassable, and there was a large breach in the western portion of the city walls, through which the conquerors passed.

The decision to make Córdoba the capital of al-Andalus seems to have come soon after the conquest. The Arabs took control of the old governor's palace and constructed a *qasr* where the Alcazar of the Three Kings stands today. The first cemetery was placed outside the city walls to the northwest. The Roman bridge and walls were reconstructed by 719-21.

With the installation of Abd al-Rahman I as the first emir in 756, the Arabs appropriated the basilica of San Vicente for a mosque, and the earliest incarnation of the Great Mosque was constructed there in 786. With subsequent remodelling and enlargement, particularly during the caliphal period, the mosque would eventually attain the dimensions of 178 x 125 m, or about 2.25 ha (about 5.6 acres), including the garden in front. San Vicente was apparently the only Christian church within the late antique city walls; the appropriation of this structure by the Arabs seems to have had the effect of pushing Christians outside the walled part of the city. A significant Christian community seems to have remained in Córdoba until at least the fall of the caliphate, particularly in a suburb around the former Cercadilla as evidenced by an episcopal ring found in the grave of an abbot named Samson, consecrated by a bishop who was in office in 862 (Edwards 2001: 226).

Meanwhile, the number of Córdoba's Muslim inhabitants increased dramatically, and suburbs (*al-rabad,* giving rise to the Spanish word *arrabal*) began forming outside the city walls as well. The earliest suburb, Saqunda, formed to the south, inside the hairpin curve formed by the Guadalquivir river southwest of the Roman bridge, and was built over a former Late Roman *vicus* (parish) called Secunda. Saqunda had the largest souk in the city and attracted wealthy merchants and artisan guilds, becoming a demographically and economically powerful element in Córdoban politics. Partially as a consequence of its growing power, Saqunda revolted in 818 against the emirate and was suppressed – many of its inhabitants were killed and the rest forced into exile, particularly to Toledo, Fez and Alexandria (Guichard 1995:44). The suburb was razed to the ground, and subsequently became one of Córdoba's largest cemeteries. In 2001-2, an extensive excavation of nearly 16,000 m^2 was carried out in a renovation of what is now Parque de Miraflores and revealed the foundations of the dense settlement that was once Saqunda (see *arqueocordoba* at www.arqueocordoba.com/visitas/2visitas/2visita-saqunda. htm).

Continuing economic growth favoured suburban expansion

elsewhere, particularly to the west and northwest. Around the periphery of the expanding city were built numerous private palaces or country estates, called *al-munya*/s, where government officials and members of the Córdoban aristocracy resided. Some of these were built over former late Roman/Visigothic country estates. One of the largest was al-Rusafa, the palace of the Umayyad family established under Abd al-Rahman I, which was built over a Visigothic palace villa called Balat Tudmir (Theodemir's Palace). This palace has been located in the suburb of Turruñuelos northwest of the city in a cultivated area, where the outlines of this large complex can (or could in the mid-1990s) be seen in aerial photographs. Ultimately, caliphal urban agglomeration around the city nucleus would consist of 11 palaces, 22 *al-muna*/s, and 12 suburbs on both the east and west side of the original walled city nucleus (Scales 1997: 177), interspersed among extensive irrigated gardens that would have supplied the city. The source of the water was the old Roman aqueduct of Valdepuentes, which has its source in the hills north of the city at Bejarano, snaking south and then east across the Guadalquivir valley to the city, passing by what would become Madinat al-Zahra on the way.

Under Abd al-Rahman II (reigned 822-52), two important state institutions were built: the Dar al-Tiraz and the Dar al-Sikka (the mint). The Dar al-Tiraz was a silk textile and embroidery workshop where embroidered robes, arm-bands and ribbons were manufactured. These articles of clothing were worn by the emir and distributed to ambassadors, district governors and foreign emissaries as political gifts. The probable remains of the Dar al-Tiraz have been located during salvage archaeological work in the vicinity of the basilica of San Zoilo, just outside the Bab al-Yahud (Jewish Gate) northwest of the city, a large building about 80 m² square with thick dressed stone foundations have been uncovered (Arjona Castro 2004). Meanwhile, the possible remains of the Dar al-Sikka have been discovered, mainly in the form of crucibles that were used to melt and pour gold, along Calle San Basílio, near the Bab Ishbilya (Seville Gate) in the southwest corner of the walled city, next to the Alcazar (Arjona Castro & Frochoso Sánchez 2002).

The establishment of the caliphate by Abd al-Rahman III in 929 involved a nearly complete reorganization of the central government, including the building of an large army consisting entirely of mercenaries and an enormous bureaucracy whose membership was drawn from outside the various competing factions he sought to suppress and integrate in the central state's fiscal structure (Barceló 1998). In this sense, the Córdoba caliphate was entirely distinct from the state structures of feudal Europe, which consisted of long chains of personal dependence from the monarch all the way down to the lowliest serf. Very probably as a consequence, the establishment of the caliphate coincides with the construction some 7 km west of the city of a separate palace and government complex covering some 7 ha called Madinat al-Zahra. This complex would contain the palace residence of the caliph, a large hall for the reception of visitors and emissaries, the chancellaries and archives, headquarters for the military with warehouses for armaments, a mosque and its associated religious personnel, the new mint, a workshop quarter for the production of state goods (such as the famous white, green and purple glazed wares discussed in Chapter 5), associated markets, and residences for all the personnel required to support these various institutions and industries (Acién Almansa & Vallejo Triano 1998: 124). Excavations on this enormous complex began in the early twentieth century and continue to the present day, although approximately 5 ha of the complex remain unexcavated.

Despite the apparent success reflected in these amazing constructions, the caliphate would last barely 90 more years. In a terrible civil war that erupted in 1009-10, the suburbs of Córdoba and Madinat al-Zahra were sacked, burned, and razed (see Scales 1994 for a complete account of this destruction) and remained buried under rubble and topsoil for the next thousand years, until the expansion of Córdoba in the 1990s disturbed them once again (Scales 1997).

3. The formation of al-Andalus

State revenues

The Islamic state of al-Andalus was a classic fiscally based society in which principal source of revenue of the central government was in the form of various taxes levied and collected on its subjects (Chalmeta 1994a). As a Muslim government, it imposed taxes differentially on the basis of religious faith. Muslims paid taxes stipulated in the *shari'a* (religious scriptures, specifically the Quran), while non-Muslims paid a *per capita* or poll tax, called the *jizya*, as well as a land tax called the *kharaj*. The tax on non-Muslims appears to have been adopted by the Arabs from standard Byzantine practice in the Syrian territories they had conquered in the mid-seventh century, which also imposed a *per capita* tax, called the *capitio*, and a land tax based on the size of a holding, called the *jugatio* (Simonsen 1988: 127). Under this system, the payment of taxes indicated that the taxpayers were under the protection (and control) of a particular city in the empire; under the Arab system, this protection, called *dhimma*, was extended to all 'people of the Book', that is, Christians and Jews, who were referred to as *dhimmi*. Barceló (1997c) estimates that the tax burden on *dhimmi* was about three and a half times that on Muslims during the emirate of Muhammad I (852-86).

Chalmeta (1994a) argues that in the case of al-Andalus, converts ceased to pay the *per capita* tax, but they continued to pay a tax based on the size of their cultivable lands, which was called the *tabl*, while at the same time becoming morally responsible for paying the *'ushr* as well. Hence, according to Chalmeta, 'it is difficult to see [the fiscal change] arising out of this conversion as representing anything more than a substitution of names: *kharaj* becoming *tabl* and *jizya* becoming transformed into *'ushr* (1994a: 747). The relatively heavy tax burden borne by the converted indigenous landholders (i.e. the *muwallads*) compared to the Arab conquerors may be one of the main factors behind the discontent that lead to rebellions in the second half of the ninth century, as Fierro (1998) has argued (see further discussion of this issue in the next chapter).

The *'ushr*, which was theoretically the only tax required of Arab Muslims, operated as a kind of income tax on produce, paid in kind, that is, in the form of measures of wheat, barley, or other agricultural produce. *'Ushr* was collected by a Muslim official. Although not specified in the Quran, *'ushr* is probably derived from the *zakat*, a kind of tithe intended as a form of alms for the poor, stipulating a tithe on the produce of cultivated lands: 5% on irrigated and 10% on dry-farmed fields. Hence, while non-Muslims paid a fixed tax (*kharaj*) based on the size of the land holding, Muslims paid a percentage of production, which suggests that if a Muslim landowner chose to reduce production, his tax would correspondingly decrease. The same would not be true of a non-Muslim landholder; this would seem to motivate the non-Muslim to maintain small landholdings at high levels of agricultural intensification. A tithe of 2.5% is stipulated on merchants' profits, which presumably was paid in coin. A further tax was imposed on Muslim men in the form of a charge for release from military duty, called *fida* or *nadd* (Chalmeta 1994a: 745). Barceló (1997c: 109) shows that the contribution of this military release was substantial, amounting to about half of all the revenues collected in coin from Muslims.

Under Malikite law, which originated in the later eighth century and became increasingly influential in North Africa and al-Andalus, conquered lands were divided into two main categories (Hopkins 1958: 30; Manzano Moreno 2006: 36-7). In one, lands conquered by force (*'anwatan*), i.e. where the populus puts up a resistance and is forced to capitulate, the inhabitants would then be subject to a *kharaj* tax (and presumably, a *jizya* as well, although this was a separate issue). This conquered land becomes the property of the *umma*, or the Islamic community at large, although in practice these funds go into the state's fisc. However, the initial Arab conquest of Hispania actually precedes the point at which Malikite law becomes influential, so the manner in which lands were divided and taxes imposed remains somewhat ambiguous.

The other possibility was for indigenous leaders and their

subjects to solicit or openly submit to Muslim rule, and to form a pact (*sulh*) with the conquerors, whereby they keep their lands and pay a *jizya*. This was apparently the case of the pact with the Visigothic count, Theodemir, discussed in more detail below. In al-Andalus, this kind of pact does not seem to have survived past the 740s, and tax collection seems to have reverted to an arrangement more like the first.

The fundamental unit of tax collection was the village community, called an *al-qarya*, or in the cases of large landholding owned by an individual, at the level of the estate, or *al-daya*. Both these terms are preserved in modern Spanish and Portuguese (*alquería/alcaria*, *aldea/aldeia*) as terms referring to villages, although the former is a historical term that usually refers to a deserted village, at least in Portuguese (see below). The amount to be paid by each community was determined by a census, and the community would then be liable for the taxes based on the census. This would theoretically create problems in cases where individuals converted (or left the community and settled elsewhere), since the community would still be liable for the tax computed on the basis of the census, increasing the per capita taxation rate for those that remained. On the basis of this reasoning, it is sometimes argued that conversions to Islam might have proceeded at the community-wide level, rapidly accelerating the process. Village communities were in turn organized into districts, called *kura,* which typically formed the hinterlands of urban settlements such as Córdoba, Seville, Málaga, Beja, and so on.

As the economy of al-Andalus grew, so did the demand and supply of goods for long-distance trade. The Córdoba caliphate became the hub of a long-distance trade network that stretched from the southern edge of the Sahara to the eastern Mediterranean. From this trade, the state was able to collect a wide range of taxes and duties, which developed into a substantial portion of the state's revenues (Chalmeta 1994a).

Based on the official tax estimates from the *kura* of Córdoba, Barceló estimates that only 15% of the tax revenues derive from taxation on commerce (Barceló 1997c: 118-19, 124). Based on this, he argues that the role of commercial activity in the development of the Andalusian economy has been greatly exaggerated. But as Chalmeta points out, the tax figures are taken from sources 'written by Muslims for Muslims' (1994a: 745) and that tax revenues outside those sanctioned by the *shari'a* were considered 'outside the law' (uncanonical) and were 'swept under the carpet in the official statistics' (1994a: 753). This may have been particularly true for revenues from customs duties on goods traded in and out of al-Andalus (*maks*). Customs duties are not sanctioned by the *shari'a*, and levying of these taxes as well as taxes beyond the 2.5% *zaqat* on commerce was considered tyranny and despotism. In fact there exists a *hadith* that specifies that the customs duties collector will burn in hell (Björkman 1987: 194), suggesting, again, that these taxes may have been difficult to talk about in official documents.

And yet rulers were known to have levied them. The prevalence and unpopularity of uncanonical taxes is particularly well documented in the North African polities. In the mid-eleventh century, when the pious fundamentalist Almoravid dynasty came into power, ultimately extending its reach into al-Andalus, one of the major factors behind their popular support was their repeal of uncanonical taxes, which included the customs duties as well as the *kharaj* which had continued to be imposed on indigenous Muslims after they had converted. Invariably, however, 'the fiscal requirements of the State would again assert themselves against religious scruples' (Halm 1996: 357), and rulers would be forced to return to their despotic policies, setting the stage for yet another fundamentalist uprising that promised to return to the letter of the Quran.

For this reason, it seems likely that taxes drawn from long-distance trade are underestimated, possibly to a considerable degree. How much revenue could customs duties and related taxes and tolls have generated? The Andalusian geographer al-Bakri, writing in the 1060s, reports that 26,000 silver dirhams per day were collected from each of the four gates into the Fatimid palace city of al-Mansuriyya in present-day Tunisia (Halm 1996: 361). Although this sounds like a rather general estimate, we can for the sake of argument calculate the yearly income from duties in this one Fatimid city (nearly contemporaneous with the peak of the caliphal period) as approximately 38 million dirhams per year, or, at an exchange rate of 35 silver dirhams to 1 gold dinar (Goitein 1965), as a little over 1 million dinars per year. During the 920s, according to Ibn Hawqal, the ruler of the semi-independent city state of Sijilmassa, the ruler received 400,000 dinars in taxes, tithes, and market dues, in duties on goods traded to and from al-Andalus and Ifriqiya, levies on caravans leaving for the south, and profits from the mint, which was striking silver coins from mines in the Atlas (Brett 2001: 254). This amount is said to have been half the total yearly revenue of the Maghreb as a whole.

The Marches

On the northern peripheries of the state's territories a frontier existed with the portions of the Peninsula controlled by the Christians (Kennedy 1996: 56-8; see Manzano Moreno 1991 for an extended treatment of the significance of the Marches). This frontier was divided into Upper, Middle and Lower Marches (see Fig. 3.1). The Lower March was centred around the old Lusitanian capital of Mérida, surrounded by the plains of the Extremadura. Its populations consisted mostly of *muwallads* (populations of Muslim converts from the earliest years of Arab rule, discussed in the next chapter) and Berbers. The Middle March was centred around Toledo. The city itself was dominated by *muwallads*, but Berbers controlled surrounded by upland plains and mountains around it. Berbers in this region as well as in the Lower March are thought to have been semi-nomadic pastoralists who retained their tribal organization and identity throughout the Umayyad period. The Upper March was focused around the Ebro river valley with Zaragoza as its capital, and was by far the most urbanized of the Marches, having (besides Zaragoza), Tudela, Calatayud, Huesca, and Tortosa, not to mention Tarragona and Barcelona, just to the north of the river, although Barcelona fell to the

Franks by 801. Here, Arab families controlled the fertile river valleys, and the uplands were controlled by indigenous Christians and powerful *muwallad* houses, particularly the Banu Qasi. Yet another peripheral area of dissidence, which was not actually a frontier, was the rugged mountainous region of the *tierras malagueñas* between Málaga and Ronda, which became the staging area for a major challenge to the state under the rebel leader Ibn Hafsun, discussed separately in the next chapter.

Although ostensibly the March regions were a frontier to be defended against Christian advances from the north, these areas developed a political dynamic of their own that had important implications for the development of the Umayyad state. For one thing, it is likely that frontier areas had some degree of fiscal immunity or independence, since they were responsible for supporting the armies and fortifications along the frontier, as well as providing hospitality for the expeditionary forces sent by Córdoba on campaigns into Christian territories. In the case of Tortosa in the Upper March, the governor was allowed to retain the taxes collected locally for use in maintaining the frontier defences, and they fiercely resisted giving up that autonomy as the central state grew stronger and attempted to regularize fiscal control throughout its territory.

Hence all three of these frontier regions retained considerable political and fiscal autonomy. The Umayyads did not even begin to exercise direct fiscal and political control over them until the 840s; even after this there was a strong tendency towards separatism, and all three of the regional capitals had to be re-subdued in the first three decades of the tenth century. The upshot of this is that central state of Córdoba faced threats not only from expanding Christian states in the north, but from the centripetal tendencies of the March regions themselves.

Vascos

Vascos is the site of a walled city on the Middle-Lower March established and occupied primarily during the caliphal period.

3. The formation of al-Andalus

It is located in the province of Toledo (Castilla-La Mancha) about 40 km southwest of Talavera on a promontory along the west bank of the deeply entrenched Rio Huso as it flows north into the Tajo just above the present-day Azután dam near the village of Navalmoralejo. Excavations were carried out at the site under the direction of Ricardo Izquierdo Benito between 1975 and the late 1980s (Izquierdo Benito 1994; 1999).

Vascos is thought to be the site of the historically documented *madina* of Nafza, the name of a powerful Berber tribe that lived in the area. However, archaeological evidence, discussed below, suggests that it functioned mainly in the interests of the central state in Córdoba, particularly in the califal period. Remains of a Bronze Age occupation have been found at the site. There was a small settlement present during the early Roman period, possibly involved in iron smelting. The site is in fact located along a Roman road, parts of which are still extant, that seems to have run west from Toledo to the important north-south road that connected Seville, Mérida, Cáceres and Léon and Astorga to the north. A piece of a carved stone church altar in the 'Visigothic' style was also recovered at the site, suggesting that the community persisted into the Late Roman period.

Located about halfway between Toledo and Mérida along the Middle March, Vascos as an Islamic settlement started out as a small *hisn* built probably during the last decades of the emirate, during the period of decline and instability known as the first *fitna* (roughly 850 to 912). During this period, Toledo was slipping away from central control and threatening to form an autonomous polity. To the west, in the region of old Lusitania, or what is now the western Extremadura of Spain and the Alentejo of Portugal, a family dynasty of *muwalladun*, called the Banu Marwan al-Jilliqi, created a semi-independent state, founding Badajoz as an alternative to the traditional capital of Mérida.

After the establishment of the caliphate in 929, a fully-fledged *madina* was founded over the site of the castle, probably some time between 930 and 950. It is possible that

Toledo and Mérida remained hostile to the central state, and the caliphate was attempted to establish a new *madina* in the region from scratch. A great deal of time and effort were expended in the establishment and construction of this city. The settlement was roughly rectilinear, about 400 m long and 265 m wide and surrounded by a substantial defensive wall of dressed stone pierced by two large city gates, one with a horseshoe arch, and five smaller entrances. Inside, the city had all the main requirements of a *madina*: at least two mosques, a *hammam*, and an *alcazaba,* or citadel, which contained the main mosque and probably the residences of the city's governor. Outside the walls were two cemeteries, on the west and south side. Near the main gate was an extramural suburb, which is thought to been the location of workshops that produced noxious wastes, such as slaughterhouses.

Vascos had an elaborate system for collecting and retaining rainwater. A series of holding tanks called *albercas* were built along a network of natural and canalized arroyos outside and uphill from the settlement, from which water could be conducted inside the walls. At least two large cisterns of dressed stone were built inside the city walls.

Two residential areas within the walls were excavated between 1983 and 1988, including one extensive area 24 x 48 m. The excavations revealed a pattern of densely packed house compounds typical of the caliphal period: drystone masonry of loosely dressed quarried stone, tile roofs, and consisting of two to three separate rooms organized around an enclosed patio. There was some evidence of continued metal working inside the city, in the form of stone moulds for casting bronze decorative objects.

Ceramics recovered in the excavation of the households were typical of the caliphal and taifal periods (mid-tenth to late eleventh centuries) and included a significant number of pieces of Madinat as-Zahra wares, the green and manganese painted white glazed wares which are thought to reflect direct ties with the caliphal government at Madinat al-Zahra, as I will discuss in more detail in Chapter 5.

3. The formation of al-Andalus

The Islamic occupation of Vascos almost certainly ended with the Christian conquest of the area, and particularly of Toledo in 1085. Three coins of the first Almoravid governors of the region were recovered, as well as two coins of Alfonso VI, conqueror of Toledo. Following the conquest, Vascos appears to have been abandoned, although parts of the citadel may have served as a frontier fort of the Christians.

Pattern of economic and demographic growth in early al-Andalus

The emiral period was a time of accelerating economic and demographic growth, despite the uneven and fitful nature of the development of the central state as a governing body. Chalmeta's (1994a) analysis of the economy of emiral and caliphal al-Andalus indicates that the population underwent a dramatic increase from the establishment of the emirate in the 750s through the time of the caliphate in the mid-tenth century. The size of the economy, as measured by state revenues, increased by a factor of 3.6 between 822 and 947, dates for which there are reasonably accurate figures for land tax revenue intake (Chalmeta 1994a: 750). This increase is due to both population increases and dramatic increases in the total amount of land under cultivation. Population follows a similar curve, growing from an estimated 7 million in 822 to about 10,200,000 in 947 (estimates are drawn from tax figures; this does not count the Christian population north of the Marches). Using the late nineteenth-century estimates of F.J. Beloch for the Roman population, Chalmeta suggests that the peak Roman period population of Iberia was 7 million, dropping to a figure between 3 and 5 million by 700 as a result of plague, economic decline and famine, then rising again to over 10 million during the caliphate. Interestingly, Europe north of the Pyrenees experiences a similar trajectory of growth at the end of the first millennium, although the really rapid growth seems to start somewhat later than in the Peninsula. Davis (1986) suggests that the population of Europe grew

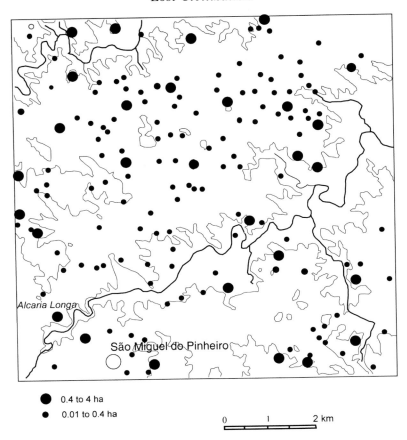

Fig. 3.4. Map of 1992 survey area near Mértola (Boone and Worman 2007) showing location of later Islamic period sites (mid-tenth to mid-twelfth century).

about 300% between 950 and 1250. The difference is that the growth spurt seems to occur 150 to 200 years earlier in the Peninsula. Also, there are several reasons to the think Iberian population went into decline following the dissolution of the caliphate and particularly after 1150 (see below), whereas northwestern Europe continued to grow up to 1250, levelled off, and declined precipitously around 1350 as a result of a new outbreak of the plague.

Very little archaeological work in the form of systematic, full coverage surveys of contiguous areas has been carried out for the medieval period in Spain and Portugal that would allow us to compare patterns of growth and decline archaeologically. Survey in the surrounding hinterlands of Mértola carried out by Boone (Boone & Worman 2007) has provided some data for the southwest corner of the Peninsula (see Figs 3.4 and 3.5). The survey revealed that some time after the dissolution of Roman control of Iberia in the fifth century, small hamlets and villages began to appear in the study area. Over the next five hundred years, and particularly following the Muslim invasion of 711, settlement density increased eightfold over what it had been during the Roman period. The survey recorded 160 Islamic period sites, consisting chiefly of scatters of building stone, roof tile and pottery ranging from 100 sq m to 4 ha.

On the basis of imbrex tile designs, we were able to distinguish between what we called a transitional period (550-950), which corresponds to the end of the Roman period and the emiral period, and a later Islamic period (950-1150), which essentially corresponds to the caliphal and taifal periods. There is no sharp or even gradual break in rural material culture signalled by the Arab conquest in this region until the mid-tenth century, which why we avoided labelling the sites late Roman or emiral, although for all intents and purposes most of them probably fall in the emiral period. From this we are able to make some tentative statements about changes in site character and distribution. At around 950 to 1000, small hamlets consisting of anything from one to three household compounds were abandoned and larger aggregated villages, exemplified by Alcaria Longa, were constructed in hilltop locations (though not very high hills – the total difference in relief in the survey area is about 150 m). However, numerous smaller sites, probably consisting of single household dwellings, small hamlets of a dozen or fewer house compounds, as well as agricultural field houses, also appear on the landscape.

Site numbers and total settlement area through time

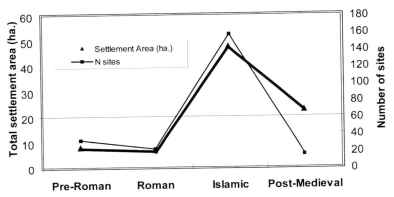

Fig. 3.5. Settlement numbers and area from the Roman to the early modern period, based on the Mértola survey.

Based on the difference between transitional and later Islamic period site numbers, it is tempting to infer a period of nearly explosive growth in settlement density at around 950-1000. However, since none of the small sites identified as Islamic on the basis of roof tile designs and surface pottery have been excavated, we cannot be sure whether the occupation of the small sites identified as later Islamic extends back into the 800s or whether many small sites continue to be occupied up to the eleventh and twelfth centuries, as do the larger aggregated hilltop sites. In all likelihood, many of the smaller 'later Islamic' sites represent a continuation of the growth of transitional period settlements discussed above, and this growth culminated in the formation of aggregated hilltop sites in the mid- to late tenth century. Fig. 3.5 shows the changes in settlement numbers and area.

Subsequently, during the mid-twelfth century, the majority of rural villages was abandoned, nearly a century before the *reconquista* in 1238. The region remained largely depopulated until the mid-late 1400s, and settlement density in the region was never again as high as it was during the later Islamic period. Geoarchaeological evidence of widespread erosion and soil loss suggests that overuse of the land may have been a factor in the abandonment.

The pattern of aggregation and shift to hilltop locations in the mid-tenth century mirrors the appearance of castles and associated villages, called the *hisn-qarya* complex, seen in eastern Spain and in Europe north of the Pyrenees (discussed in detail in the next chapter). However, none of the village settlements in the Lower Alentejo of Portugal have associated fortifications and there is essentially no evidence of a *hisn-qarya* pattern, as it is understood in eastern and southern Spain, despite the argument of Argemi Relat et al. (1993) that one existed at Alcaria Ruiva, a village located about 15 km north of the survey area, which will be discussed in more detail in the next chapter. The abandoned eleventh- and twelfth-century villages of this region, which are quite numerous and visible on the ground, are known locally as *alcarias* (a cognate for Spanish *alquería*, derived from the Arabic *al-qarya)*. In the Alentejo of Portugal, the term refers specifically to the ruins of deserted villages which local inhabitants are aware were Islamic period settlements (i.e. '*sítios dos Mouros*'). Some of the more extensive ruins are noted as *alcarias* on the mid-twentieth-century *Cartas Militares*, topographic maps that record a wealth of local toponymic lore reflecting a cultural landscape that has now all but disappeared. Some modern villages in the area are named after nearby ruins, e.g. the modern village of Alcaria Longa, located about 1.5 km from the site discussed above.

Salvatierra Cuenca and Castillo Armenteros (1991) carried out survey and excavation of emiral period rural settlements on an 8 x 5 km area in Campiña de Jaén (Jaén), a wide section of the Guadalquivir valley between the Sierra Morena and the Sierras del Prebético. The study area, ranging in elevation from 400 to 600 m, is located just northwest of the highway from Jaén to Baeza, and borders the south bank of the Guadalquivir. This area was the location of numerous salt works (*salinas*) from at least Roman times to the sixteenth century.

The survey revealed 18 Roman sites from the first century, some of which seem to be clearly associated with salt production, and others which are more likely agro-pastoral in nature. By the third century the number of settlements had dropped to three. The fifth to the seventh centuries are a blank, although the investigators allow that the dearth of clearly diagnostic ceramics from this period may be a factor. In the eighth and ninth centuries, seven small village or hamlet sites appear on the landscape, dominated by a site located on the southwest slope of the Cerro de Peñaflor, at 637 m the highest point in the study area. Salvatierra and Castillo identify this settlement with the Berber settlement of al-Mallaha, an *alquería* mentioned in the *Muqtabis*, a historical text of the *taifa*-era historian Ibn Hayyan. The extensive excavations at the site of Cerro de Peñaflor revealed courtyard houses and a system of interconnected underground chambers carved into the bedrock that served as cisterns, discussed further in Chapter 5. In the late ninth and early tenth centuries, this area becomes the focus of the central state in Córdoba, which was attempting to consolidate its power, and the Berber tribes that were settled in the region. The old Roman capital of the region, Mentisa (now La Guardia) was abandoned and a new Islamic provincial capital was founded at Jaén. Rural settlements in Salvatierra and Castillo's survey area were completely abandoned, and new rural settlements do not reappear there until the late twelfth century. Hence, the pattern of settlement here is roughly parallel to that found in the hinterlands of Mértola.

Similarly, the settlement surveys of Reynolds and Gutiérrez Lloret, discussed in Chapter 2, show a pattern of settlement increase during the caliphal period. Gutiérrez Lloret's (1989) work at the mouth of the Segura river shows that during the period immediately after the establishment of the caliphate, the highland sites that had been characteristic of the emiral period started to be abandoned, and settlements associated with what would become extensive irrigation systems in the lowlands and marshes throughout the later medieval period began to be established (see Fig. 3.6).

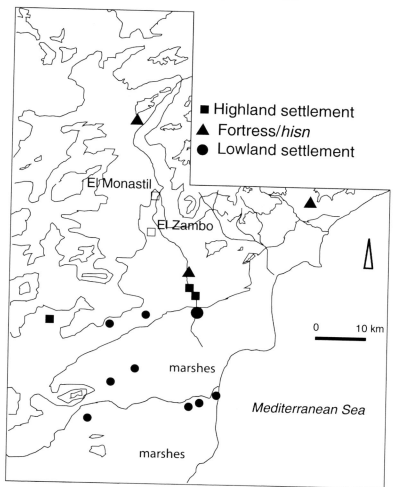

Fig. 3.6. Emiral and caliphal period sites (eighth to late tenth/early eleventh century) in the the lower Vinalopó and Segure river valleys, showing the degree of resettlement of lowland irrigated lands and the mouths of the two rivers during the caliphal period (redrawn and combined from Reynolds 1993: fig. 112 and Gutiérrez Lloret 1989: fig. 4). Several highland fortresses, like El Zambo and the fortress at El Monastil, are abandoned during or after the establishment of the caliphate.

In the following chapter, I continue discussion of rural settlement and rural sites and their relation to the social organization of al-Andalus, a subject that stands at the centre of a debate over the nature of continuity and rupture between the late Roman and the Islamic period.

4

Tribal collectives or feudal lords?

The appearance in the tenth and eleventh century of castles and towers, and the subsequent formation of villages around them, is perhaps the most visible feature of Europe on the threshold of the High Middle Ages. In the late 1970s the historian Pierre Toubert (preface, Bazzana et al. 1988; Toubert 1973; 1990) offered a wide-ranging explanatory model for the appearance of this pattern, which he termed *incastellamento*, his term for the reorganization of European settlement around hilltop fortifications, or castles, which imposed feudal dominance on dependent villages within their jurisdiction. In his view, castles had a social function beyond just simple military utility: they 'contained habitat and organized landholding' (Glick 1995: 13, paraphrasing Toubert). One of the main attractions for anthropologically oriented archaeologists of the early medieval period was Toubert's insight that fortifications were not just responses to historical contingencies like Viking raids or attacks from Central Asian nomads, or the result of serendipitous innovations or inventions like the mott and bailey, but rather the archaeological signature of a new social structure: feudalism. Pierre Guichard was apparently struck by the similarity between *incastellamento* in Europe and a similar and contemporaneous pattern of castles and villages in al-Andalus. Guichard's model, however, held that the basic building block of Andalusian society was the tribe or segmentary lineage, not the dyadic relationship between lord and vassal characteristic of feudal Europe. In the early 1980s, working in conjunction with the archaeologist André Bazzana, he outlined a programme of research to

95

explore further the relationship between tribal organization and Andalusian *incastellamento*.

The Guichard model and the *hisn/qarya* complex

As we saw in Chapter 1, Guichard had sought to demonstrate once and for all that the Arab invasion and subsequent Islamic period in the Iberian Peninsula represented a sharp break in historical tradition rather than a passing foreign occupation that was quickly assimilated and Hispanicized. Coming from the *Annales* tradition of historiography, he tried to show that the Islamic period marked a sharp break in *mentalités*, mental structures and modes of consciousness and representation in the past that shape historical process. Drawing on structural-functionalist theory in social anthropology, Guichard argued that the Islamic and Latin Christian civilizations were based on opposing structural principles of organization in the domestic domain. These were reflected in differences in systems of descent (patrilineal vs. bilineal) and the organization of kin groups (corporate descent groups vs. bilateral kindreds). Drawing on Murphy and Kasdan's (1959; see also Sahlins 1961) discussion regarding the functional implications of Bedouin kinship and sociopolitical organization, Guichard argued that segmentary lineage organization facilitated the defence, expansion and growth of these groups once they arrived in the Peninsula (Guichard 1976: 257), dominating and replacing indigenous groups and ways of life. Barceló (1990: 107) has taken this idea much further with his oft cited idea '*el ambiente tribal produce tribus*' (the tribal environment generates tribes). This is essentially an implication of the old British structural functionalist position that kinship and descent systems are mental structures that determine how labour is organized and social reproduction is achieved in the absence of centralized systems of authority. It assumes that tribal (read 'primitive') peoples have no other means of organizing themselves in the absence of more hierarchical systems of dependency available under feu-

4. Tribal collectives or feudal lords?

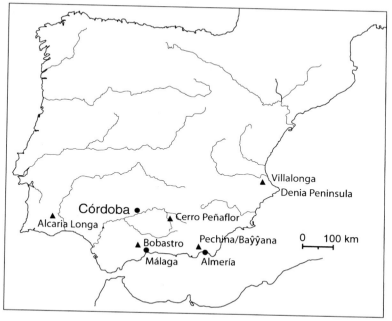

Fig. 4.1. Map of Iberian Peninsula showing the location of sites discussed in Chapters 4 and 5.

dal or slavery modes of production, which presumably existed under the Visigoths and Hispano-Romans in the late Roman period. Hence social reproduction outside the context of the clan or tribe would be impossible, since there would be no one to marry and no one to organize collective labour with. I will return below with a critique of this position.

Three important elements of Guichard's tribal model have implications for the archaeological record of the transition between late antiquity and the Islamic period (Manzano Moreno 2006: 129-46). First is Guichard's basic assumption that segmentary tribal organization was the key building block of Andalusian social structure. If this is the case, then segmentary organization should leave a recognizable archaeological signature, which, as we see below, Guichard and his archaeological colleagues have argued exists in the system of castles and associated villages called the *hisn/qarya* complex. Second is the insistence that Arab and Berber tribes were essentially egalitarian, at least in the sense that land was communally held among tribesmen. This would contrast sharply with land-holding and territorial organization of feudal Europe, characterized by unequal relationships between lords and individual tenant farmers, and reinforces the idea that Islamic society represented a sharp break in historical tradition. The egalitarianism of Arab and Berber tribes has also been a key element in the interpretation of *husun* as refuges for villagers rather than the seats of powerful lords or chieftains. Finally, Guichard's view that segmentary organization implies strict endogamy – specifically the patrilateral parallel cousin as a preferred marriage partner – would have been strong enough to have prevented cultural syncretization between Arab/Berber immigrants and Peninsular natives, and thus allowed 'oriental' structures to expand at the expense of previously existing Western traditions.

French archaeologists André Bazzana and Patrice Cressier, working with Guichard (1988), have attempted to operationalize Guichard's hypothesis concerning the cultural and demographic processes by which Islamic culture became implanted on the Iberian cultural landscape by focusing on the relationship between castles – termed *husun* (sing. *hisn*) in Arabic – and the surrounding hinterland composed of small villages, or *alquerías*. In doing so, they attempt to delineate a functional connection between Guichard's structural model and Toubert's concept of *incastellamento*.

In an introduction to Bazzana, Cressier and Guichard's *Les châteaux ruraux d'al-Andalus* (1988), Toubert argues that while the *hisn/qarya* complex was not specifically feudal in nature, it had a chronological and functional similarity to the castle and village complex of the Christian world. In contrast to Europe north of the Pyrenees and Italy, where *incastellamento* refers to a system in which hinterlands were organized and controlled by a seigniorial (i.e. feudal) regime, Bazzana, Cres-

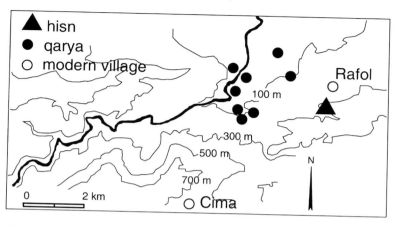

Fig. 4.2. Map of *hisn/qarya* association at Villalonga (Valencia) in the Denia Peninsula about 80 km south of Valencia (redrawn after Bazzana et al. 1988: fig. 151).

sier and Guichard view the Iberian *hisn/qarya* complex as the expression of segmentary tribal organization that, as explained above, is a key element of Guichard's original hypothesis concerning how Islamic culture became established in Iberia. Under this system, the inhabitants of the *alquerías* would presumably be free of any feudal-type obligations to a regional lord or *qaid*, and held and farmed lands collectively and on a relatively egalitarian basis. The *hisn*, in turn, was, at least in its tenth- and eleventh-century manifestation, a fortified refuge built and maintained by the tribal collectives as protection in times of disorder, not as a means of implementation of control by a higher authority.

The *hisn* consisted of a citadel which typically contained the household compound of a *qaid*, who was an administrative representative of the state who collected taxes and organized the defence of the surrounding cultivated lands, and a walled enclosure, called an *albacar*, which was used a place of refuge for inhabitants of the surrounding villages (Glick 1995: 20-1). Typically, an average of seven to ten *alquerías*, or villages, pertained to each *hisn*, such that they used the fortress as a refuge and paid taxes to its administrator. According to the model (see Cressier 1991), villagers would be freemen with no feudal obligations to a lord. They were tribesmen who held lands communally and farmed them collectively. Thus the *hisn/qarya* complex does broadly resemble the *incastellamento* system envisioned by Toubert, in that the castles 'contain habitat and organize landholding'.

The tax collection system described here is what is generally known as *iqta'*, often called 'tax farming', a system that is sometimes referred to as 'Islamic feudalism'. The appointed collector, called a *muqta'*, receives a concession to collect taxes from a given locality, pays himself with a portion of the proceeds, and passes the rest on to the state. As we will see below, the appointee might well be drawn from the local tribe from whom the taxes are to be collected, or from tribes or military units from outside, as in the case of the *junds* in mid-eighth-century al-Andalus. Wickham (1985) has pointed out that feudalism and *iqta'* are similar in many ways, and the differences can be subtle. There are several different forms of *iqta'*, just as there is variation in the specific arrangements under feudalism, and some forms are closer to what might be called feudalism than others. Table 4.1, based on a discussion by Lacoste (1974), outlines and compares some of the main features of each system.

It is easy to see why Wickham argues that *iqta'* and feudalism are similar in that they represent a movement toward localization of power, and a shift in the focus of power toward that tied to land. A *muqta'* in a tax farming system could easily turn into a local regional lord if he becomes too powerful. He might rather easily manipulate the portion of tax he keeps relative to the portion turned over to the state, although often the amount was agreed upon first under the terms of the concession. In some areas of the Middle East, *iqta'* concessions became hereditary later in the medieval period. It is easy to imagine the concessionaires using their proceeds to buy lands and establish their own estates in the manor of feudal lords. At this point, whether a *muqta'* actually owns the property rights to the lands and labourers he collects tax from is largely academic.

4. Tribal collectives or feudal lords?

Fief	Iqta'
Beneficiary (of a fief) owes allegiance to a higher lord	Beneficiary (of the *iqta'*, called a *muqta'*), owes allegiance to the central ruler
Beneficiary receives, with definite title and in a specific location, a portion of political authority over each peasant	Beneficiary receives delegated and temporary right to extract taxes from a named tribe, village, or locality
Receives a share in the rights of ownership of the land	No rights over land which continues to belong either to the state or to the tribe that has the usufruct
Beneficiary receives property rights, political, juridical, and administrative rights, and economic rights over his lands and the peasants who live on it	No additional rights in the government or administration of tribesmen
Each peasant in a direct relationship of dependence with his master	Each peasant a member of his tribe

Table 4.1. Comparison of feudalism and *iqta'*, or tax farming (based on Lacoste 1974).

Whether and to what extent an *iqta'* system was implanted in al-Andalus, as well as the specific terms of its implementation there, are poorly understood, since there are very few documents describing what was going on there in the first two centuries after the Arab conquest (see discussion in Scales 1994: 120-31; also Chalmeta 1994b). Some scholars, such as Scales, argue that the Arabs simply adapted the pre-existing Visigothic scheme of tax and rent extraction to their own needs, while others, like Wickham (2005: 101, following Manzano Moreno 2006), argue for the importation of a new system, coinciding with the settlement of the *junds* as tax collectors. It is quite possible that both occurred.

Bazzana et al.'s programme strongly implies that the *hisn/qarya* complex constitutes of itself evidence for segmentary lineage organization and that in contrast with the situation in feudal Europe during the same period, it reflects an egalitarian arrangement in which lands were held communally by the tribesmen (see e.g. Bazzano, Cressier and Guichard 1988: 35). In contrast, Azuar Ruiz (1982: 40) has argued that the *hisn/qarya* complex represents an implementation of local control by a *qaid* who acted as a representative of centralized urban-based state. In some cases, these *qaids* may have attained such power and independence as to become 'true Muslim *señores*'.

This argument, however, does not exclude the possibility that organization at the local level was tribal in nature. Acién Almansa (1989; 1998: 362-3) has presented a similar view, arguing for an ongoing dynamic of interaction between immigrant Arab and Berber groups, who were tribally organized, and indigenous people who had developed a protofeudal organization in the period just prior to the invasions. Acién Almansa further argues that tribal organization could well also have been a social adaptation of converted indigenous populations (*muwalladun*). This is a critical point that to which I return later in this chapter.

Toponyms as evidence for tribal settlement

An ancillary source of evidence for extensive Arab and Berber settlement in the hinterlands and for segmentary organization in general comes in the form of numerous Berber and Arab place names, particularly those in the form of the toponym which includes the prefix Beni- (meaning 'descendants of' in Arabic) and often paired with a name derived from a particular Berber or Arab clan or confederation. For example, Benicasim is derived from Banu Qasim, a group of Kutama Berbers from northern Morocco (Glick 1995: 31). Beni- place names are quite numerous in the eastern and southeastern areas of the Peninsula; they are also common in Algeria and Morocco.

Another line of evidence for Arab and Berber settlement comes from tribal registries, such as the one included in the chronicle written by Ibn Hazm, a mid-eleventh-century Arab historian (Scales 1994: 24-5), which lists immigrating Arab and Berber clans and indicates where they settled (Taha's 1989 history is based on such registries). Yet this document was written down nearly 300 years after the initial settlement was supposed to have taken place.

The toponymic and tribal registry evidence has not gone uncontested. Criticism has taken two general forms (Collins 1994: 139; Glick 1995: 24). First, much of the tribal documentation was actually written down hundreds of years after initial Arab and Berber settlement is generally held to have taken place in the eighth century. The later Islamic period was a time of intense political conflict during which claims to land rights that dated back to the initial settlement were reinforced with claims to pure Arabic, Berber and *muwallad* descent. Hence these histories may well have been constructed in order to subvert competing claims to land rights and legitimacy to power while reinforcing the significance of the historian's or his patron's own claims.

Secondly, while the Beni- place names may well indicate initial Arab or Berber settlement in the early period, the names tell us nothing about whether tribal organization of villages continued unchanged through the succeeding centuries of Muslim dominance, or whether intermarriage and cultural assimilation between migrants and indigenous peoples occurred. That is, Beni- place names may provide evidence for the foundation of land claims by Arab and Berber groups in the formative period, but they do not tell us whether these groups were organized as segmentary lineages, or how far into the later medieval period they retained such organization. Furthermore, *muwallad* families adopted Beni- or Banu- appellations tied with Hispano-Roman or Germanic names, such as the Banu Qasi

103

(sons of Cassius) of the upper Ebro valley, the Banu Karluman, the Banu Longo, the Banu Angelino, the Banu Gharsiya (i.e. García), the Banu Martín, etc. (Chalmeta 1992). Are we to assume that these groups also adopt segmentary lineage organization and a clan logic that prescribes strict endogamy, or did they simply adopt the naming system and retain a more European form of elite family structure, such as the 'house' or '*lignage*' described by Jack Goody (1984)?

Are Berber and Arab tribes isomorphic?

By far the most numerous ethnic contingent among the initial conquerors were the Berbers. These were tribally organized groups indigenous to North Africa. The first group of conquerors of the Peninsula in 711 was predominantly Berber. Led, as we have seen, by Tariq ibn Ziyad, the Berber governor of Tangier, who was the client, or *mawla*, of Musa ibn Nusayr, the Arab governor of Ifriqiya, centred in Qayrawan, the force numbered probably 7,000-12,000 men. It is difficult to believe that after the initial invasions many more Berber settlers would not have streamed across the Straits to join their kinsmen (the same could be said of the Arabs immigrating from the Mashriq), in a manner similar to the way the Anglo-Saxon migrations are thought to have played out in southern Britain. However, there seems to be little direct documentary evidence for this kind of migration pattern.

There is continuing debate over the extent to which the Berber and Arab warriors would have brought their families, indeed their whole tribes with them on the initial campaigns. Guichard (1976; 1994: 683) and Barceló (pers. comm.) have argued strongly that they did, and in fact Guichard cites the Lombard historical observer, Paul the Deacon, who describes Muslims moving into southern Gaul in around 720 'with their women and children', although he was writing some 40 or 50 years after the fact. The addition of the Berber conquerors' families would increase the estimated number of immigrants by a factor of at least three or four and further bolsters

4. Tribal collectives or feudal lords?

Guichard's argument that Arabs and Berbers coming into the country with their family groups intact could and would have remained endogamous, self-contained family or tribal units that would have resisted assimilation by the large indigenous majority. Manzano Moreno (2006:166-86) is less sure, and has presented a sustained argument against the idea that tribal organization continues for long in the Peninsula.

The Berbers that settled initially were from large tribal confederations settled in the northern and central regions of Morocco, including the Rif Mountains and the central plains. Some or most of them had probably already undergone conversion to Islam before arriving in the Peninsula, but most had not yet become Arabized – they retained their Berber language and possibly some aspects of their original material culture (Manzano Moreno 2006: 170-2). Berbers also settled in urban areas as clients (*mawali*) of the Umayyad elite, and became scholars, administrators and legal specialists.

The debate over the tribal nature of the incoming Arabs and Berbers comprises at least three more or less opposing views. The first is the one taken by Guichard and held by the historian and linguist Miquel Barceló, as well as the archaeologists André Bazzana and Patrice Cressier. In their view, Arabs and Berbers entered the Peninsula organized as segmentary lineages and retained this organization for at least several centuries following the invasion. The second view is that Arabs and Berbers may have at one time been characterized by this kind of tribal organization but that it rapidly broke down as they settled under new circumstances in al-Andalus, such that it is of relatively minor importance in understanding the structure of Andalusian society (Manzano Moreno 2006: 129-53). A third view, which I outline in more detail below, is that segmentary lineage organization is largely the figment of mid-twentieth-century structural-functionalist anthropologists' imaginations (Kuper 1982; Munson 1989), and that it is therefore of little use in understanding how and why Arabs and Berbers became so firmly established on the Peninsula.

Much of Guichard's evidence regarding lack of importance of

intermarriage between Christians and Muslims in creating a kind of impermeable structurally opposed Arab culture in al-Andalus comes from genealogical sources that pertain to a rather small Arab urban political elite, while his general conclusions regarding the overall importance of clan endogamy in the rural hinterlands are entirely based on analogy with recent historical Bedouin ethnographic descriptions. As I will discuss in further detail below, there is no reason to think that Berber social and territorial organization resembled that of Bedouin pastoralists of the Arabian Peninsula. In Murphy and Kasdan's (1959) formulation, and in segmentary lineage theory in general, a Bedouin segmentary lineage is 'a genealogically structured group in which the economic and political rights and duties of individuals are, to some degree, determined by their membership in corporate descent groups' (Munson 1989: 388). The desert nomads of Arabia are endogamous, the preferred marriage partner being a patrilateral parallel cousin, or father's brother's son or daughter. These lineages herded livestock as corporate groups, holding the herds, which are a mobile resource dependent on spatially ephemeral and patchy grazing, as a collective. Endogamy, and specifically patrilateral parallel cousin marriage, kept herds within closely related patrilineages.

When the Arab tribes conquered the settled Byzantine lands of northern Syria and established themselves in cities, palaces and fortresses, they retained their old Bedouin kinship and marriage patterns even though these patterns had become disconnected from their original function in pastoral subsistence. Patrilateral parallel cousin marriage took on a purely symbolic significance, and was considered crucial to retaining the purity of the ancestral line. This pattern followed Arab immigrants to al-Andalus, but it is very likely that it began to break down as the Arab families were dispersed and settled into sedentary agriculture across the Peninsula. Peter Scales (1997: 116-31) has found indirect evidence of this breakdown with reference to the Marwanids, one of the original *baladi-yyun* lineages of al-Andalus and the family of the subsequent

4. Tribal collectives or feudal lords?

Umayyad ruling dynasty. Scales points out that in Ibn Hazm's eleventh-century genealogical compilation and history of the Umayyads, the *Jamharat ansat al-arab*, Ibn Hazm makes repeated references to the Umayyads' 'exhaustion' or 'dying out'. Yet the genealogies show the Marwanids producing tens of sons and hundreds of grandsons – how could they be dying out? Scales suggests that this is simply a reference to the fact that the Marwanids stopped practising strict patrilateral parallel cousin marriage, hence the lineage is, in Ibn Hazm's view, becoming increasingly sullied, impure and diluted. Scales suggests that the abandonment of the endogamic marriage pattern was due to the sedentary, dispersed nature of Arab settlement in al-Andalus, which made endogamic marriage both economically irrelevant and practically inconvenient. Like Manzano Moreno (2006: 149), Scales sees the faction – a group of allied individuals with overlapping political and economic interests, as the most salient social grouping in the formation of al-Andalus. Hence, vis-à-vis the Arabs, we cannot depend too much on the idea of endogamy constituting a barrier to cultural syncretization in Andalusian society.

What can we say about Berber tribal groupings? One problematic aspect of Guichard's use of an idealized tribal model is his implication that Arab and Berber tribal organization was isomorphic. This, in fact, was a view widely held among Middle Easternist social anthropologists from the 1950s to the early 1980s; the segmentary lineage model was considered to be broadly applicable to Middle Eastern, North African and Sub-Saharan African tribal peoples like the Nuer and the Dinka (see Kuper 1982 for a critique of this view, especially pp. 90-1). In an article entitled 'On the Irrelevance of the Segmentary Lineage Model in the Moroccan Rif', the social anthropologist Henry Munson (1989) argued that the typical Berber tribe of the region did not conform to the segmentary lineage model in any way. Munson focuses his argument around a detailed ethnographic study of the Aith Waryaghar by anthropologist David M. Hart (1976).

The Aith Waryaghar are a sedentary agricultural Berber-

107

speaking group on the northern slopes of the Moroccan Rif. Their history as a group extends back to the earliest Islamic conquest of the region in the eighth century. Indeed, one of the earliest Islamic urban foundations in Morocco, Madinat en-Nakur, was located near the centre of their territory in the valley of al-Hoceima and served as the capital of a small client state of the Córdoban emirate until the mid-ninth century, when it was destroyed by the Fatimid expansion (Boone et al. 1990; Pellat 1992). Although the Aith Waryaghar probably converted to Islam around the time of the foundation of Nakur, they continue to speak a Berber dialect. Although it is likely the Waryaghar have undergone some organizational changes since the early medieval period, they would seem to constitute about as ideal an ethnographic analogy for the kind of Berber group that settled al-Andalus as any that currently exists.

The Waryaghar are one of a number of territorial groups, termed *dhiqba'ir*, that live in the Moroccan Rif. The term *dhiqba'ir* is a Berber cognate for the Arabic word *qabila*, which in turn translates into the anthropological term 'tribe'. *Dhiqba'ir* were in turn divided into *rbu'*, or quarters or sections. For the Waryaghar, however, these terms refer strictly to contiguous territorial units, not genealogical groupings. In the classic segmentary lineage model, genealogical groupings and territorial units are considered to be isomorphic, and here is where the problem arises.

Munson argues that in his original analysis, Hart consistently attempted to impose the segmentary lineage model on the territorial organization of the Rifian tribes where in fact in did not really fit. In Hart's view, *dhiqba'ir* constituted a genealogical unity as a tribe, or group of clans, and the *rbu'* constituted clans within the *dhiqba'ir*. The clans were further subdivided into individual agnatic lineages, termed *dharfiqin*. Hence, for Hart, the territorial division and subdivision of Rifian tribal lands were 'nothing more than the lineage system spread out spatially on the ground' (Hart 1976: note 20; cited in Munson 1989). Munson, however, makes a strong and convincing argument that tribal divisions in Rifian society were

108

4. Tribal collectives or feudal lords?

fundamentally territorial divisions, not simply territorial reflections of genealogical organization.

First of all, Munson shows that Rifian *dharfiqin* (i.e. clans and lineages) were dispersed among territorial units; related lineages rarely resided on contiguous lands, as in the classic segmentary lineage model. Secondly, clans never acted as corporate groups in the defence of their lands or in any other subsistence-related or political activity. Munson shows that land was generally held by individuals as private property (*mulk*) and could be bought and sold by individual tribal members – land was not held communally by a descent group. A neighbouring landholder was more likely than not to be a member of a different patrilineage. Furthermore, most tribe members were unable to trace their ancestry beyond three or four generations – it just wasn't that important to them in their day-to-day life. Land was held privately and passed on in equal shares to sons, with daughters receiving a half share, in line with Maliki law. As a result, brothers and sons of brothers in effect become each other's closest competitors, and violence leading to murder most often arose among close agnatic kin over rights to land. This is in contrast to the segmentary lineage model where violence is famously held to be directed outward from a lineage or clan. Marriage, rather than being endogamous, was most commonly out of the family group, better to form alliances and combine land holdings with other families.

Tribal groupings were headed by councils of factional leaders called *imgharen* (sing. *amghar*). At the lowest level, *imgharen* were leaders of joint or extended family groups, but very powerful *imgharen* led much larger factions that included genealogically unrelated allies and their families. In fact, *imgharen* preferred to ally with men with whom they would not be in direct competition for inheritance, i.e. not with agnatic kin. These factions, called *liff*, were generally named after the lineage name of their leader, but the tribesmen who were under his influence were not all of the same lineage. *Liff* were the fundamental building blocks of Waryaghar tribal organization, not patrilineal descent groups.

109

The *imgharen* held weekly councils in which they settled disputes, imposed fines on murderers, and carried out other legal judgments. Significantly for our argument above regarding tax farming, or *iqta'*, as the articulating factor between the central state and local tribal producers, successful *imgharen* could be appointed as tax collectors for the sultan. In fact, Munson notes that there was intense competition among *imgharen* over these appointments. Hence tax collectors were drawn from the tribal groups themselves, not brought in from the outside, further undermining the argument that tribal organization was essentially egalitarian or communal.

To summarize, the Aith Waryaghar certainly reckoned kinship along agnatic lines, but patrilineal descent was not the organizing principle of collective action, and patrilineages were not the basis of corporate groups. The term for tribal group is a cognate for the Arabic term for clans, but Berber clans were not corporate descent groups that held land communally, and endogamy was not in any way a preferred marriage arrangement. Rather, territorial contiguity and propinquity of landholdings were much stronger underlying factors in tribal solidarity. In Kuper's words, 'People's behaviour was not governed by principles of kinship and descent, and their strategies could not be captured by rigid models of descent theory. Social systems all had to allow room for manoeuvres and manipulation. Normal people were motivated by self-interest. Communities were not elaborated ideological constructs, they were competitive associations of individuals making a living as best they could in a particular landscape ... The classic anthropological opposition was between blood and soil. Lineage theory assumed blood is paramount ...' (1988: 208)

Archaeology and the *hisn/qarya* complex

One of the most significant implications of the *hisn/qarya* model was that it called for a kind of archaeology that had never been practised before in the Iberian Peninsula, at least for the medieval period: extensive, or, as it is called in the

4. Tribal collectives or feudal lords?

British tradition, landscape archaeology. In the investigation of *incastellamento* in al-Andalus, Toubert called for a programme of periodization of castles, a typology of fortifications in terms of form and function, and a focus on the relationship between castles and villages and their associated irrigation systems (see his preface to Bazzana et al. 1988: 10). To this end, André Bazzana, Patrice Cressier, Pierre Guichard, and in a slightly different vein, Miquel Barceló and his research group extensively documented the *hisn/qarya* complex in the eastern and southeastern part of the Peninsula particularly in the areas around Valencia, Alicante and Almería (Bazzana et al. 1982; Bazzana et al. 1988; Cressier 1992; 1998a; b).

The programme was met with resistance on several fronts by other Spanish archaeologists and Arabists, some of whom argue for a more feudal arrangement, at least in some regions of the Peninsula (see Bazzana et al. 1988: 38-43; Glick 1995: ch. 2 for reviews of these critiques). Indeed, the idea that *incastellamento* is reflective of both feudal regimes on one hand and segmentary tribal organization on the other seems problematic at the outset, particularly in view of the fact that Guichard sees them as structurally opposed at the most basic level. Given the underlying similarities discussed above between feudalism and *iqta'* as systems of surplus extraction, the common denominator may be simply the localization of power in the absence of a strong central state apparatus, although the problem of timing specifically in the tenth and eleventh centuries, rather than earlier, still needs to be addressed. The fact that *incastellamento* is almost precisely coeval in both Christian and Muslim Europe suggests something more general is behind this phenomenon.

In any case, with respect to al-Andalus, there are really two questions to resolve here: first, is the *hisn/qarya* complex the archaeological signature of Arab and Berber tribal settlement, and second, is it the archaeological signature of the kind of segmentary lineage organization described by Guichard? Strictly speaking, if the answer to the first question is positive, then *hisn/qarya* units should appear on the Iberian landscape soon after the initial Arab and Berber invasions, and they

111

should appear everywhere on the Peninsula where Arab and Berber groups settled. We might also expect to see the *hisn/qarya* pattern established in areas from which these groups had originated. In fact, none of these conditions is satisfied *per se*.

There are fortifications of various kinds dating to all periods of the Middle Ages and castles show considerable chronological diversity in location and function, as might be expected, since fortifications are built for many different proximal purposes. As we saw in the previous chapter, at the very beginning stages of the conquest, the conquering armies built garrisons that retained the place name based on the Arabic term *qala* (fortress), as in the modern cities of Calatayud or Calatrava (Acién Almansa 1999). Fortifications are known to have been built along the southern Atlantic and Mediterranean coast by the emir Muhammad I following a rash of extremely damaging raids by Danish Norsemen in the 840s. The coastal fortress of al-Marya, which formed the nucleus of the later city of Almería, is an example (see the discussion of Pechina in Chapter 5).

Acién Almansa (1989; 1998) has argued that many of the hilltop fortified settlements in eastern and southeastern Spain that date to the time of the Arab conquest were founded not by immigrating Arab or Berber tribes but by slaves or serfs who had escaped the feudal control of their lords in cities and landed estates of the late Roman period. These foundations are distinguished toponymically by having retained Latin place names into the Islamic period; for example, settlements with names beginning with *Munt-* (*monte*) or *Sant-* (*santa/o*). Acién Almansa argues that these fortifications were later reused as strongholds for *muwallad* rebels attempting to gain independence from the Córdoban emirate during the crisis period of the late ninth and early tenth centuries, as in the case of Bobastro, discussed below.

Even for the castles firmly identified as *husun* and shown to be associated with *alquerías* established during the Islamic period, the timing is not quite right. None of the castles documented by Bazzana et al. (1988: 296-7) date to earlier than the

4. Tribal collectives or feudal lords?

mid-ninth century, and many date to the mid-tenth at the earliest. The *alquerías* themselves appear not to have been securely dated; it would be interesting – in fact crucial – to know whether the village foundations precede the castles or vice versa. Elsewhere, Azuar Ruiz (1989: 411-23) has shown, based on an extensive settlement survey in the Denia Peninsula (southern Alicante), that *incastellamento* does not occur there until at least the end of the tenth century, too late to account for the Berber migrations of the eighth century. Furthermore, the construction of castles continues into the eleventh to thirteenth centuries, and seems to be tied to deliberate defensive policies implemented by the Almoravid- and Almohad-controlled central state, not to local tribal organizations. Hence Azuar argues for a widening of Guichard's hypothesis into a perspective that would admit that the *husun* may have functioned in any one of a number of sociopolitical ways, depending on the period and prevailing local social and economic conditions, a point on which Bazzana et al. (1988) agree.

Hence the mid-ninth to the mid-tenth century dates are 150 to 200 years too late to signal Arab and Berber settlement *per se* – that is, Arab and Berber settlement might be necessary to explain these new foundations (or it might not, in some areas), but it is not sufficient to explain the timing of the appearance of *husun*. The timing in fact coincides with the crisis of the mid-ninth century discussed in Chapter 3, and culminates in the establishment of the Córdoba caliphate under Abd al-Rahman III in 929 (it also coincides precisely with the earliest appearance of *incastellamento* in Italy – in 920-40, according to Toubert (preface to Bazzana et al. 1988: 12). Thus the sudden appearance of fortifications might well be interpreted as a response to the central state's increasingly intensified efforts to draw outlying areas into its orbit, particularly if the *husun* are indeed associated with the establishment of *qaids* whose role it is to collect taxes from surrounding villages.

The *hisn/qarya* model also fails the geographic distribution requirement: they should be found everywhere in the Peninsula where Arab and Berber settlement took place. In fact, the *hisn/qarya* association appears to be limited to irrigated lands (see Fig. 4.2). Furthermore, it seems to be limited to the irrigated lands of southern and eastern al-Andalus, including the Sharq al-Andalus, Alicante and the Guadalquivir valley. It is absent in the vast irrigated stretches of the Tagus and Sado rivers of Portugal. In the dry farming areas, which take up a majority of the land area of the Peninsula, the particular association of small rural castles and associated villages is also absent (see discussion of Alcaria Longa, in southern Portugal, below). It is also absent in the Balearic Islands, even though Arab and Berber settlement is known to have occurred there; *alquerías* are present, *husun* are absent. On the other hand, castle-village complexes appear in northern Castile during the first third of the tenth century in what is clearly a feudal context and where it is certain there was no Arab or Berber tribal settlement (Martín Viso 2006: 168)

Glick (1995: 21) argues for the universality of the *hisn-qarya* model in the Peninsula (i.e. outside the eastern and southern core area discussed above) largely on the basis of Argemi Relat et al.'s (1993) argument that there was a *hisn* at the settlement of Alcaria Ruiva, in the Lower Alentejo of Portugal. There is an artesian spring at this settlement that has supported a limited area of irrigation agriculture from at least the Islamic period, and it is one of the few settlements in the *concelho* of Mértola for which there is documentary evidence for continuous settlement from Islamic times to the *reconquista*. But there is in fact no trace of a fortification there from any period, and the whole argument that there was a *hisn* rests on the fact that the ribeira that drains the spring is called Ribeira de Alvacar. *Albacar* was a term for the enclosure inside a *hisn* where the inhabitants of nearby villages could gather for protection during times of unrest. But *albacar* is also a still-used Portuguese term for an enclosure for livestock. The argument that this toponym belies the presence of a *hisn* during the emiral or caliphal period depends on the assumption the term had survived intact from the Arabic to its Portuguese cognate, even though the castle itself had disappeared completely.

114

4. Tribal collectives or feudal lords?

Finally, as Bazzana et al. (1988) themselves point out, the *hisn/qarya* complex is virtually absent in northern Morocco, where the kind of segmentary tribal sociopolitical organization they envision must have existed in the medieval period and continued to exist into the early twentieth century. Hence, regardless of whether segmentary tribal organization constituted a salient feature of rural Andalusian society in the medieval period, the appearance of the *hisn/qarya* complex still needs to be explained in terms of response to social and political conditions that existed in the Peninsula itself.

Archaeological evidence for tribalism

I argued above that feudal and *iqta'* systems had some broad similarities, the principal one being that both systems entailed rent- or tax-collecting intermediaries installed more or less permanently out in the countryside, rather than centralized in the cities, such that we see the 'translation of public obligations [i.e. taxes] into relationships of personal dependence, and the association of these with landholding' Wickham 2005: 99). There are some salient differences between the two systems, however. In the feudal system, each peasant farmer is tied by a unique chain of dependency relations from the local lord to the regional lord, all the way up to the monarch. In the *iqta'* system, the chain of dependency goes down only as far as the tribal group (Crone 2003: 155-9; Lacoste 1974). Taxes were collected on a *per capita* basis from the local group, but the group as a whole was responsible for coming up with the tax to be handed over to the local collector, who could be a *qaid* or beneficiary of an *iqta'*. There is strength in numbers, which would imply a significantly increased bargaining power on the part of the tribe in contrast to the individual serf, from whom rent could be extracted to the maximum extent by local lords (Pettengill 1979). Put simply, Middle Eastern and especially North African tribes had more political autonomy as groups vis-à-vis the central state than did their peasant counterparts in feudal Europe. In this sense, Barceló (1990: 108) is correct in saying that tribal organization is an alternative to central government (or the *sultan*) – tribes can govern themselves and can be expected to press for as much political autonomy from the state as they can get. In traditional Morocco, this variable autonomy was behind the *bilad al-makhsan/bilad as-siba* dichotomy (which was really more of a continuum), in which some lands, or tribes, were under regularized control of the central government (*al-makhsan*) and paid regular taxes, while others were dissident (*siba*) and resisted taxation.

If tribal organization was present on the landscape in al-Andalus, how would we recognize it? What is needed is the development of more specific archaeological correlates that would distinguish tribal organization, as opposed to proto-feudal and feudal organization. I would suggest that the enhanced autonomy of tribes, as opposed to feudal peasantry, should be reflected in material culture in a couple of important ways. First, drawing on analogy with North African Berber tribes, political autonomy is reflected in the continuing right to bear arms. Weaponry is often highly ornate, suggesting a symbolic as well as utilitarian importance. Secondly, I have argued that display of personal jewellery represents, among other things, a strategy by which agro-pastoralists converted surplus accumulated during good years into durable form (silver), and that this durable wealth was retained by the primary producers themselves rather than extracted in the form of rent by dominant landowners. This pattern of personal adornment is commonly observed among women of the tribally organized Berbers of Morocco and Algeria, where it constitutes a signal of a family's wealth and prosperity, and is not the kind of personal, publicly displayed wealth normally associated with dependent peasants of feudal Europe.

This autonomy is reflected in several ways. I have argued (Boone 1994; 1996) for autonomous, tribal organization in the Lower Alentejo of Portugal based on archaeological evidence recovered at the caliphal and taifal period site of Alcaria Longa (Boone 1992; 1993; Boone & Worman 2007). Radiocarbon and ceramic evidence from Alcaria Longa indicates that these set-

4. Tribal collectives or feudal lords?

tlements were occupied from about 950 for the next 150 to 200 years and then abandoned some time around 1150, nearly a hundred years before the conquest of the area by the Portuguese Christians in 1238.

In this region the production regime was one of extensive agro-pastoralism rather than the intensive irrigation agriculture characteristic of the coastal region of eastern Spain and the Guadalquivir valley. Faunal remains preserve very poorly in the region due to acidic soil conditions, but a preliminary analysis of 225 bone elements recovered at Alcaria Longa indicated the presence of sheep/goats (69.7% of individual specimens), cattle (13.2%), deer (2.6%), rabbits/hares (2.6%), and dog (2.6%), as well as two elements of quail or partridge; there were no wild or domestic pig remains. Macrobotanical analysis carried out in the past year revealed burnt olive leaves and wood. Whole and fragmentary circular hand-powered millstones for grinding cereals are numerous at the site, and are frequently found on the surface of other Islamic period sites.

Excavations carried out between 1988 and 1994 at the late Islamic period village site of Alcaria Longa revealed a village consisting of about 35 multi-structure house compounds covering 1.6 ha. The primary occupation of the site began c. 950 to 1000 and the site was abandoned around 1150. A locally produced roof tile recovered from one of the house compounds was incised with a brief inscription in Arabic (Boone 1996: Fig. 8), implying that the villagers were Arabic speakers and writers, although not necessarily that they were Muslims. A silver Arabic coin minted in the name of Ibn Qasi, the Sufi rebel leader of Mértola from 1141 until his violent death in 1144 (Antunes & Sidarus 1993) was found on the floor of one of the house compounds, along with two silver rings with glass stones. The coin and its context may date the approximate and abrupt abandonment of the site, which is corroborated by the radiocarbon evidence. The coin had been perforated with two holes for wear as jewellery in the manner, for example, of historic Moroccan tribes, where perforated coins and other forms of silver jewellery are worn on a daily basis by women. In

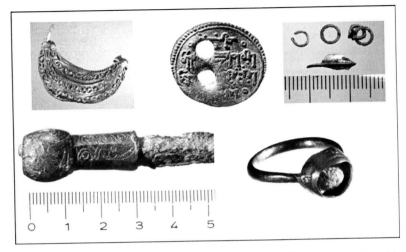

Fig. 4.3. Evidence that the inhabitants of Alcaria Longa (Mértola) stored wealth in durable form and displayed it in the form of personal adornment. At the lower left is a decorated bronze pommel of a dagger hilt – evidence of personal weaponry.

general, the excavations revealed a relatively high incidence of silver jewellery, including an additional perforated coin, a silver filigree earring, pieces of a silver chain, and stone beads recovered from depositional contexts indicative of loss during use (i.e. while being worn). Additionally, an ornate bronze dagger hilt was recovered from the floor levels of one of the household compounds, indicating the use of ornate personal weaponry.

One does not ordinarily expect to find this kind of elaborate personal adornment and weaponry in the artifact assemblages associated with dependent peasantry of early medieval Europe, or at any time during the Middle Ages. Its presence at Alcaria Longa suggests that this population was somehow able to retain a significant portion of its surplus and convert it into durable form, a practice that suggests a higher degree of political and economic autonomy than is usually found in subject peasantry paying rent on the lands they farm. It is possible that the inhabitants of Alcaria Longa were organized as some kind of tribal arrangement similar to that found up to the twentieth century in rural Morocco, where women conspicuously wear silver and other jewellery in part as a social indicator of their family's stored wealth. The wider distribution of this pattern in rural al-Andalus awaits further confirmation through excavation of a larger sample of settlements, and will require extensive excavation of household clusters, with the use of fine screening of floor deposits. In any case, Alcaria Longa offers a tantalizing example of how archaeology can provide evidence for social organization at the rural level, not often found in the documentary record.

Muwallads and proto-feudalism

The question of the existence of feudalism in the Visigothic period and its survival into the Islamic period has been such a contentious, emotional debate in Spain and Portugal mainly because it is so inextricably tied to issues of national narrative. For the traditionalists, the survival of feudalism constitutes evidence for continuity and for the assimilation and Hispanicization of the Arab invaders. On a more theoretical level, there was in the late nineteenth and twentieth centuries a strong belief that passing through a feudal stage was a necessary prerequisite for the development of modern European nation states. If Spain had no feudalism, then it couldn't be a fully functioning modern state on a par with the rest of Europe. This kind of thinking is a relic of the old provincial Spain (i.e. why is Spain different, what's wrong with it?) and has pretty much evaporated with the post-Franco economic development and the formation of the European Community, in which there is no question about Spain's status with the rest of Europe.

Acién Almansa's *Entre el Feudalismo y el Islam* (1997) in many ways constitutes the last gasp of the old style debate regarding the role of feudalism in Visigothic and Islamic Spain. Acién Almansa focuses his argument around the case of Umar Ibn Hafsun, discussed below, and argues that Ibn Hafsun's

119

revolt against the Córdoba emirate in the late ninth and early tenth centuries constitutes the last battle between the feudalism of the Visigothic society and the new order imposed by the Arabs. Acién Almansa suggests that Ibn Hafsun was consciously invoking the feudal arrangements of his Visigothic ancestors, converting back to Christianity in the process, and calling for a return to the old order.

From about 852 to 912, the Andalusian state suffered a crisis that resembled in some ways the *taifa* period of the eleventh century following the dissolution of the Córdoba caliphate, although in this case the central government did not completely disappear (Kennedy 1996: 63-81). In several parts of the Peninsula, the central power in Córdoba was contested by Arabs, Berbers and *muwalladun* living on the periphery of Muslim territory. In the Marches, where Arab control was tenuous, converted Muslims, probably allied with Mozarabs as well, constituted a kind of hegemony. In the Lower March, in the region of old Lusitania, or what is now the western Extremadura of Spain and the Alentejo of Portugal, a group of *muwalladun* called the Banu Marwan al-Jilliqi actually created a semi-independent state with a capital in Évora, Portugal, as an alternative to the traditional capital of Mérida. Another peripheral region was the rugged mountainous area behind Málaga, where an independent polity contested emiral power under the leadership of a *muwallad* named Umar Ibn Hafsun.

The *muwalladun* are usually characterized as the descendants of indigenous Christian families who had converted to Islam (Chalmeta 1992), although Fierro (1998) has suggested that at the beginning it may also have denoted those who had adopted Arabic lifestyles and language through clientage. The term may further denote landholding families in the hinterlands that had converted early on in relationships of clientage, and distinguished themselves with the later *musalima*, or 'new Muslims', who converted spontaneously, i.e. 'old money' vs. 'new money'. In general, however, they were non-Arab Muslims in a Muslim community controlled by an Arab elite. As such, they were looked down upon and prevented from rising to the

120

4. Tribal collectives or feudal lords?

highest levels of civil and military government and they were probably taxed at a higher rate than Arabs despite their having converted to Islam, as discussed above in Chapter 3.

Out of this situation developed the more specific, contextualized definition of *muwallad* in ninth-century Andalusian society as provincial renegades and rebels. They appear on the scene as a political force a few generations after the Muslim occupation and the subsequent conversion of their parents or grandparents, particularly during the mid-900s, and they disappear a few generations later, once they have been fully integrated into Andalusian society, during the first fifty years of the Córdoba caliphate. Chalmeta (1992: 807) notes that when the caliphate fell apart in 1009, the resulting fragmentary *taifa* states were lead by rival factions that included various Arab factions, Slavic clients and Berbers, but there was not a single *muwallad*-led *taifa* state. It is possible that *muwallad* status again became important during the second *taifa* period between the Almoravid and Almohad control of the Peninsula, as in the case of the Sufi rebel leader Ibn Qasi of southern Portugal (Goodrich 1978), who led a local revolt against the expanding Almoravid state.

The biographies of *muwallad* rebels such as Ibn Hafsun, discussed in detail below, make it clear that their rebellion against the Umayyad central state is motivated by their treatment as second-class citizens by the Arab elite or their clients and by their resistance to the Córdoban state's increasingly effective tax collection protocol, specifically with regard 'to their right to share power and compete for economic and social rewards on equal basis with the Arabs' (Fierro 1998: 311). In these concerns, the *muwallads* found a kind of solidarity with the Mozarabs (the Arabized Christian minority), and they sometimes acted in concert during rebellions. Some popular accounts have seen in this seemingly unholy alliance evidence that the *muwallads* were attempting to return al-Andalus to a Christian or Visigothic past, but in fact their common beef was against the Arab controlled Umayyad state, not against Islam itself.

Ibn Hafsun and Bobastro

Bobastro was the hilltop fortified capital of the famous rebel leader Umar Ibn Hafsun, who led a revolt against the nascent caliphal government in Córdoba between 879 and 917 (Fierro 1998; Martínez Enamorado 2007; Wasserstein 2002). During this period the Córdoba central state was renewing its attempts to regularize tax collection in the provinces, and this turned out to be the trigger behind rebellions all around the margins of the territory of al-Andalus. These rebellions cut across ethnic and religious lines, and included *muwallads*, Christians and possibly Berbers, all of whom were united against Córdoba's attempts to collect what they viewed as excessive taxation, or more specifically, higher taxation rates than their Arab and old family compatriots. Local leaders like Ibn Hafsun built strongholds, which were also called *husun*, from which they could exercise control over an area of dependent villages and towers, often passing their power from father to son.

Umar Ibn Hafsun was said to be a member of a landed *muwallad* family in the vicinity of Ronda who claimed descent from a Visigothic count or magnate named Alfonso three generations back; the family had converted to Islam in the early years of the 800s. In 879 he killed a neighbour in a feud, was disowned by his family and fled to Morocco. He returned a year later and established himself as a bandit leader in the wild mountainous region east of Ronda, having given up claims to his lands in Ronda, and starting again from scratch.

Ibn Hafsun established his base of operations at Bobastro, an impregnable hilltop fortress overlooking the Rio Guadalhorce. The region is characterized by limestone karstic geology and has numerous voluminous Artesian springs that water extensive irrigated fields and gardens. Dry farming of cereals was also practised in the lowlands. The area was ethnically diverse during the Islamic period, having been settled by Arab *jundis* (contingents of the Arab army commanded from Damascus, who had settled in al-Andalus with grants of land in the

122

4. Tribal collectives or feudal lords?

mid 700s, discussed in Chapter 3), as well as by Berber tribes during the earliest years of the Muslim occupation (Martínez Enamorado 1996; 2003). There appears also to have been a substantial Christian population that remained unconverted and took refuge in the area after the occupation, fleeing lands taken over by the Arabs, as evidenced by at least three churches known from the site.

Ibn Hafsun survived a series of Umayyad expeditions against him in the 880s but was ultimately persuaded to surrender and sent to Córdoba where he was forced into the army, in which, somewhat ironically, he served in campaigns against the Banu Qasi *muwallad* rebels on the upper March. But Ibn Hafsun was said to have been rebuffed by his Arab superiors and mocked as a neo-Muslim, and he deserted and returned to Bobastro, this time as a leader of a rebel principality. Ibn Hafsun apparently won the support of local inhabitants, who included both Christians (or Mozarabs) and *muwallads* like himself, with promises of protecting them from excessive taxation and forced labour by the central state. His influence widened, possibly extending from Cartagena to the Strait on the coast, and inland to Écija and Jaén, an area that fairly closely parallels what would become the kingdom of Granada from 1250 to 1492. The limits of this kingdom are defined by rugged mountains with narrow irrigated valleys that are relatively easy to defend from outside attack. At one point, Ibn Hafsun led a raid right up to the walls of Córdoba itself, about 160 km to the north.

In 899 Ibn Hafsun is said to have converted to Christianity. Yet by 910 he was receiving ambassadors of the nascent Shiite Fatimid state centred on what is now Tunisia (and the former Carthage), and it was later claimed that he adopted Shi'a Islam (Martínez Enamorado in press; the Umayyads were Sunni). One chronicle of the period reports that Friday sermons were said in the name of the Fatimid caliph al-Mahdi in all the mosques of the towns that supported Ibn Hafsun. Yet another chronicler says that Bobastro was the headquarters of the Christians and contained a great number of churches, convents

123

and basilicas, and mentions no mosques. In fact, three churches have been partially excavated on the site (Martínez Enamorado 2004), but no mosque has yet been located. The possibility exists that Muslim rites were performed in what we would call Christian churches.

Recently, Wasserstein (2002) has argued that Ibn Hafsun's genealogy is in fact fabricated. Wasserstein argues that no other contemporary genealogy beside Ibn Hafsun's has its generational depth – eight generations, including Ibn Hafsun himself. Furthermore, no Andalusian *muwallad* genealogy follows its ancestors back more than one generation before the family's conversion to Islam. In marked contrast, Ibn Hafsun's putative genealogy extends back four Christian generations to a count named Alfonso. Wasserstein argues that the invention must have occurred at some point after his conversion to Christianity in 899 and before his acceptance of support from the Fatimids in 911, his motive being to emphasize his Christian roots in order to gain wider Christian (Mozarab) support. Fierro (1998), for her part, introduces the possibility that his conversion was itself a later fabrication designed to defame Ibn Hafsun further as an enemy of the state, which ironically would set the stage for his national hero status in yet later Spanish historiography. Yet another possibility is that Ibn Hafsun was not of Hispanic origin at all, but rather a Berber who invented the genealogy to gain support of the local *muwallads* (Martínez Enamorado, pers. comm.).

The Córdoba emirate besieged Ibn Hafsun and his dependent strongholds almost continuously, but he ultimately died a natural death in Bobastro in 917. His sons continued his rule over the rebel state, but eventually quarrelled and were forced to surrender in 927. The caliphate constructed an alcázar on the site, but this was little more than a symbolic gesture, as the site had little political or economic importance to the central state after it surrendered. It was occasionally used as a summer retreat by Almoravid and Almohad elites during the twelfth and thirteenth centuries, and by Granadan leaders up until 1492. After the fall of Granada, the site was never again reoccupied.

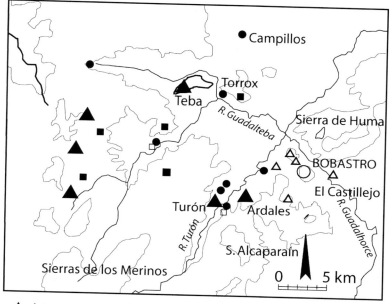

▲ *hisn* **■** *watchtower* △ *guard castle for Bobastro*

● *qarya* □ *qarya refuge tower*

Fig. 4.4. Map of Bobastro (Ardales, Málaga) and its surrounding region showing the pattern of *husun* in the area surrounding Bobastro (redrawn after Martínez Enamorado 1997: fig. III).

The site of Bobastro today is situated on a high, relatively flat mesa surrounded by sheer cliffs two to three hundred feet high. On a high point on the west end of the mesa are the remains of an alcázar measuring about 50 x 50 m. Exposed walls show clear signs of caliphal style stone construction. Hence, the fortification we see today is likely the one built by the Umayyads after the surrender in 927. The rest of the mesa is covered with the remains of dense habitation construction. On the southwest side of the site there is a small recent country house occupied by the landowner. Additionally, at the extreme west end of the mesa, about 15% of the site has been destroyed by the construction of a water collection and storage tank in the 1970s.

Bobastro is surrounded by five small *husun al-abwab*, or guard towers, that protect the approach to the site (Martínez Enamorado 1996). In the valleys around the site there is documentary and archaeological evidence for about half a dozen *alquerías* associated with irrigation systems that in many cases are still in use. The El Castillejo fortification is of particular interest because it has been tentatively identified by Virgilio Martínez Enamorado as the historically documented site of Taljayra. During the siege against Bobastro, the Umayyad forces took control of Taljayra and rebuilt it as a 'showcase' *madina* or model city – a kind of propaganda tool to persuade the rebels to submit. According to documentary sources, the Umayyads would have set up an attractive market and abundant supplies of food, and perhaps cloth, pottery and other products to demonstrate to the starving rebels the rewards of living under the umbrella of caliphal rule. A similar showcase city, called *Madinat al-Fath*, or 'City of Victory,' was built during the same period outside the walls of Toledo in a similar attempt to force the submission of that besieged rebel stronghold (Torres Balbás 1998: 278). Taljayra is in fact clearly visible from the walls of Bobastro and inhabitants would have been able to view activities at the fortress below. Taljayra is known to have been rebuilt under the direction of Abd al-Rahman II al Mundir who also directed the construction of the City of Victory outside Toledo, as well as the Umayyad alcázar at Bobastro after its surrender.

Conclusions

The near simultaneous appearance of complexes of castles and villages in both feudal Europe and eastern al-Andalus in the early to mid-tenth century seems in many ways to ask too much of the equifinality proposed by Bazzana, Cressier and Guichard (1988) – i.e. that such structures could be the signature of both feudal and tribal organization. Their contempora-

4. Tribal collectives or feudal lords?

neity would seem to point to some larger underlying historical process that remains to be completely explained. Such an explanation would tell us why the *hisn/qarya* complex existed in some parts of the territory but not others.

Tribal organization may well have been present in some parts of rural al-Andalus, although probably not of the kind invented by social anthropologists in the mid-twentieth century. It is even possible that tribalism re-emerged among indigenous peasant populations either spontaneously or through enculturation from Berber tribes. Tribal re-emergence during this period has been argued for other parts of Europe after the dissolution of Roman state apparatus, for example in early medieval Wessex (Cunliffe 1993: 266-96). But there is no reason to think that tribalism was the dominant social formation of the rural hinterlands of al-Andalus, even at the beginning.

Structures of dependency broadly resembling those of feudal Europe almost certainly existed in al-Andalus as well, but they do not constitute evidence of historical continuity with the Visigoths *per se*, rather a pattern of parallel development and convergence of forms of landscape organization that both the Europeans and the Arabs inherited from their Roman imperial predecessor. Wickham (1985: 184) has argued that tributary systems, i.e. systems in which extracted surplus moves upward to a public fisc controlled by the central state, have an almost inevitable tendency towards feudalization as state officials (various kinds of tax collectors) gain local power at the expense of the state. This appears to be exactly what we see happening around the Marches and in the *tierras malagueñas* of al-Andalus.

5

Islamization

Islamization is the most commonly cited cultural process employed to describe the gradual, fitful, but ultimately sweeping changes that occurred in the two to two and a half centuries following the Arab conquest. On the face of it, this suggests that the principal mechanism in this change was the imposition of Islamic rule by the Arabs and the conversion to Islam by indigenous Hispano-Romans and Goths. As I will outline in this chapter, the problem is not so simple: Islamization itself is composed of several intertwined influences and process involving Arab identity, religion and, just as importantly, common Byzantine and late Roman heritage between Hispania and Syria.

The parable of the horseshoe arch

Hugh Kennedy (1998: 53) has pointed out what may be a key factor behind the 'distinctness' of the formation of al-Andalus in the context of western medieval Europe: that both Syria and the Iberian Peninsula were highly urbanized former colonies of the Roman empire, and both came under Muslim control at the end of the late Roman period; Syria in 636 and Spain in 711. The first episode of Arab state formation occurred when Arab tribes conquered Byzantine-controlled Syria and established their first capital in Damascus. Since these were essentially desert pastoral tribal organizations undergoing their first experience in state-craft and empire formation, they understandably drew upon examples set by their predecessors, particularly the Byzantine and Sassanian states. These include the Arab system of patronage (Crone 1987) and the combination of land tax and *per capita* tax levied on protected non-Muslims (Simonsen 1988). Barceló (1998) has suggested that the ceremony involving the presentation of the caliph to emissaries and visitors, in which the caliph is partially hidden from view, was adopted from a Byzantine model.

In any case, by the time the Arabs initiated their conquest of the Iberian Peninsula both the conquerors and the conquered had, to varying degrees, common Roman colonial and urban backgrounds. While one had an eastern Roman background and the other western, it is also true that much of the eastern and southern coast of Iberia had been under Byzantine control for most of the sixth century. Not only that, but Iberia had had strong, nearly continuous ties with the eastern Mediterranean as far back as the orientalizing period of the Iron Age, in contrast to Europe north of the Pyrenees, a point to which I will return below. This state of affairs has some obvious implications for teasing apart what constitutes continuity and what is change in the formation of al-Andalus: the conquerors brought with them cultural elements and forms of organization that were already present in the conquered lands, and that had a common origin. This is what I refer to as convergence.

The tripartite Roman public baths are a good example of a feature common to both conquerors and the conquered, which has a common source. Public baths were a ubiquitous feature of Roman urban life throughout the empire. In the western empire, the baths declined and disappeared after the fifth century; in the east, their use continued and they were subsequently adopted by Arabs, apparently in the early stages of the development of their empire, and, with an added religious significance, became an essential feature of Muslim urban life. Hence the tripartite bath was reintroduced to Iberia after a hiatus of perhaps three centuries.

A more complex and subtle example of what we might call recursive cultural influence is reflected in the origin and spread of the horseshoe arch. The horseshoe arch is the veritable trademark of Islamic civilization in Spain and Portugal,

Fig. 5.1. Representation of a horseshoe arch with Corinthian columns on the tombstone of Andreas, dated 30 March 525, from the Basilica, Rossio do Carmo, Mértola, Portugal.

brought to al-Andalus by the Umayyads from north Syria. Yet both representations and elevations of this arch form are found in the late Roman Peninsula well before the Muslim invasions (the discussion that follows is drawn from an old and seldom cited article by Dewald 1922). The earliest representations are found on funeral stelae from Léon in northwestern Spain and date to the second or third centuries AD. Some of these stones contain stylistic elements that are found later on 'Visigothic' stone carvings, and continue into the late Roman period. Later examples of representations of horseshoe arches are found carved on tombstones. One of the best known is the tombstone of Andreas, a cantor of the church of Mértola (Alentejo), Portugal, who died in March 525 (Fig. 5.1). This shows a horseshoe arch supported by a 'twisted cord' column with Corinthian capitals, features that would carry on through the Visigothic and Islamic periods.

130

5. Islamization

Some have argued that mere representations of horseshoe arches and the actual arches are not equivalent, and don't necessarily indicate cultural transmission of the form, but actual arches are found in late Roman churches such as San Juan de Baños (Palencia), San Pedro de la Nave (Zamora), São Frutuoso de Montelios (Braga). All these churches appear to date to the mid-600s. Earlier examples are occasionally found in southern France and in Italy (for a full listing of all known examples, see Dewald 1922).

The horseshoe arch actually seems to have originated in northern Syria, and is found in both plan and elevation in Christian manuscripts, tombs, monasteries and churches. A few examples are found in Asia Minor and Egypt as well. Dewald sees the Eastern stylistic influence on Spanish religious architecture as resulting from a special connection Spain and Portugal had with Syria and North Africa. The Spanish church maintained a distinct cult independent of Rome well into the eleventh century, when Cluniac influence began to spread from north of the Pyrenees. The legend that St James travelled from the East and introduced Christianity to Spain may be seen as reflecting this special relationship. These religious ties seem to have followed long-distance trade between the eastern Mediterranean and Iberia. Dewald collected nearly forty epitaphs of merchants or colonial officials from Syria and Asia Minor. These epitaphs tend to appear in urban centres along the two main axes of commercial activity in late antique Hispania noted by Manzano Moreno (2006: 240-1): one going north from Seville through Mérida up to León, the other along the eastern Mediterranean coast.

Unlike the tripartite public bath, which suffers a hiatus in Hispania of at least three centuries before its reintroduction by the Arabs, the horseshoe arch appears to be used in the late Roman and Visigothic tradition right up to the point at which it is introduced again by the Arab conquerors, where it may well have re-influenced Mozarab church builders in places like Bobastro. In fact it continues its own pre-Muslim tradition in the Christian north and finds its way into Carolingian usage in

131

the eighth and ninth centuries. For his part, Dewald uses the late classical period sources of the horseshoe arch to underscore the idea of the assimilation of Visigothic culture into the Roman world of Hispania, a position I defended in Chapter 2: 'after the establishment of the Visigothic kingdom, the church was sufficiently powerful not only to maintain itself against the efforts of the new rulers to convert it to their Arian heresy, but also actually to convert the Visigoths to the orthodox Spanish faith. The so-called Visigothic church ... is merely the continuation of the old Spanish church, which had maintained itself in spite of two centuries of Visigothic hostility' (1922: 325).

For the Spanish traditionalists the Umayyad use of such decorative elements as horseshoe arches, Corinthian style columns and capitals, and various floral motifs, were a clear indication of continuity between the Visigothic and the Islamic period. However, most investigators now view this common usage as a parallelism, in which these traits were transmitted from a common ancestral source, Byzantine and proto-Islamic Syria.

In the last fifteen years, a new perspective on the chronology of the Visigothic churches of the central Meseta has emerged with Sally Garen's (1992) article on the church of Santa María de Melque, located about 30 km west of Toledo. Garen argued that this church, which had traditionally been dated to about the mid-seventh century, was actually constructed after the Arab invasion, during the reign of Abd al-Rahman I (756-88). Hence the church was not Visigothic at all, but Mozarabic. Subsequently, the Spanish archaeologist Luis Caballero Zoreda seems to have undergone a kind of conversion experience upon reading the article, in which Garen strongly criticizes Caballero's previously 'Visigothist' interpretation of the church, where he had carried out excavations in the 1970s. Caballero has now broadened the argument to claim that most of the churches of the Meseta that had previously been designated as Visigothic period constructions should in fact be dated to after 760 (Caballero Zoreda 1997; 2000). This position has come to be known as the non-Visigothist theory. In some cases,

5. Islamization

Caballero argues that a church may originally date to the pre-Islamic period, but was remodelled in its present form later, as in the case of San Juan Bautista de Baños, located near Palencia, which carries an inscription commemorating the Visigothic monarch Recceswinth commissioning its construction in 652 or 661. He has further suggested that a couple of secular buildings, the courtly villa of Pla de Nadal (discussed in Chapter 2) and what is almost certainly a third- or fourth-century Roman villa at Torre-La Cruz located near Alicante should also be dated to the emiral period (see comments on these designations in Gutiérrez Lloret 2000).

As Caballero (1997: 248-51) points out, the redating of these structures to the emiral period drastically alters our interpretation of the Visigothic period. First, taking away the churches makes the material record of the Visigothic period even more ephemeral. The Spanish church must be interpreted as having undergone a profound eclipse during the sixth and seventh centuries, only to flourish again under Arab dominion, during a time when all documentary evidence suggests the Muslims had passed laws against new construction or repair of Christian churches (Garen 1992: 301). All the decorative elements in these churches must be interpreted as inspired by Islamic sources; it becomes Mozarabic art rather than Visigothic or late Roman art. It also suggests that a strong vibrant Christian population remained in al-Andalus under Arab rule, which gives the whole argument what one might call a 'neo-traditionalist' cast, in line with Javier Simonet's late-nineteenth-century work on the Mozarabs. However, this position has not been enthusiastically received by other Spanish archaeologists. A symposium held in Mérida in April 1999 produced some fairly resounding opinions in favour of retaining the 'Visigothist' chronology (Arbeiter 2000; Azkarate Garai Olaun et al. 2000; Gutiérrez Lloret 2000).

My interest in the example of the horseshoe arch is in the 'parallelism' model because it suggests that many aspects of the material record of late Roman and Islamic period Iberia might be subject to the same kinds of common influence and convergence, making archaeological analysis of continuity and rupture highly problematic. Below I discuss some of the processes of change and continuity that have been proposed to accompany the transition associated with the formation of al-Andalus.

Conversion as a mechanism of Islamization

In-migration and subsequent demographic and cultural replacement figured strongly in at least the earliest versions of Guichard's argument. The fact is, however, that there were at least several million indigenous inhabitants of the Iberian Peninsula at the beginning of the Islamic period. Hence some attention must be paid to the issue of how they figure in the subsequent formation of al-Andalus as a society.

The conversion of indigenous Iberian populations in al-Andalus finds its most balanced and elegant treatment in Richard Bulliet's (1979) 'curve of conversion' model. Based on the concept of innovation diffusion, Bulliet argues that the rate of conversion to Islam was determined foremost by the probability of exposure of Muslims to non-Muslims. Hence at the beginning of the Islamic period, when there were relatively few Muslims in relation to non-Muslims, the rate of new conversions was low as a result of the low incidence of contact between individuals of the two groups. But as more conversions occurred, the probability of new conversions increased as well, and the rate of conversions began to increase exponentially. This shift to an exponential phase appears to have occurred in the mid- to late ninth century. Eventually the majority of the population converted to Islam, leaving a permanent religious minority of Christians and Jews. Hence the 'curve of conversion' follows a typical logistic path. Using dated genealogies and other literary sources, Bulliet calibrated the curve of conversion in al-Andalus by monitoring changes in the incidence of Hispano-Roman and Arabic names through time.

Bulliet's model has not figured strongly in directing Peninsular research into Islamization. Guichard (2002: 67-8) suggests that the timing of the curve is wrong, probably because there are historically deterministic, rather than random, processes involved in the process of conversion as well, such as the fact that the tax load is much lower for Muslims. Wasserstein (1985: 226) has pointed out that Bulliet's curve applies to only a specific fraction of the population of al-Andalus, i.e. those families who would end up being recorded in written genealogies, not to the population at large.

As Glick (1995: 60) has pointed out, conversion to Islam in the medieval period was not mere religious conversion, but 'social' conversion as well, involving the adoption of Arabic language as well as Islamic cultural practices. Hence, to the extent that these new practices are reflected in material culture, the conversion model, whatever shape its curve might take, may well lend itself to operationalization in archaeological terms. As suggested above, in areas were Islamization involved the conversion of indigenous populations, some everyday aspects of domestic material culture, such as utilitarian ceramic forms and production techniques, house construction and cooking practices might be conservative and show considerable continuity. Others, more closely tied to Muslim practice, such as the separation of male and female activities (i.e. household spatial organization) and food-serving practices (vessel forms associated with communal presentation of food) would be altered.

The problem that arises is that there are really two, possibly three, enculturation issues to deal with here: one involving adoption of specifically ethnic cultural practices (i.e. Arab or Berber) and the other, adoption of Islamic cultural practices. This adds considerable complexity to the problem, as indicated in the examples below.

Arabs and Arabization

The Arabs constituted a conquering nomadic tribal elite that attached itself as a political superstructure to a fully functioning bureaucratic state in Byzantine Syria. As Crone (1980: 49) points out, Islam in the first centuries was an 'ethnic faith' and the connection between being Arab and being Muslim was very strong. Until at least the mid-eighth century, essentially the only mechanism by which a non-Muslim could become a Muslim was through the institution of patron-clientage. That is, in the early period, a non-Arab's conversion to Islam necessarily entailed becoming a client, or servant (*mawla*, pl. *mawali*) of an Arab tribesman. A non-Muslim could become a client without converting, but converting did not exempt one from client status; you remained attached to the patron at whose hands you had converted. Similarly, freed slaves who converted became clients of the former masters. The relationship was therefore based on a difference in ethnic identity: an Arab was never the *mawla* of another Arab, but a *mawla* could become almost an Arab by adopting Arabic language and way of life. In this sense, Islamization was in many ways more a process of Arabization, which included adoption of not just the religion, but the social and political norms and the language of the Arabs as well.

Crone (1980) argues that the Arabs remained a formidably aloof ethnic elite, particularly in the area of religion, and impermeable to the cultural influence of the Byzantine and other bureaucrats they incorporated into the service of their state. However, in the East, where the Arab state first formed around the capital of Damascus, the system of clientage must have been the principal means by which the lifeways (such as the use of Roman style baths), techniques (such as architectural styles and building techniques, pottery manufacture) and institutions (including the institution of clientage itself) of settled urban life permeated Arab culture. There is no other way to explain how the Arabs went from tent-living nomads to dwellers in the largest and most opulent cities of the world at that time.

The institution of clientage was particularly important to the power structure that developed around the emir or caliph himself. This special relationship offered these rulers soldiers, guards, commanders and bureaucrats who had no link to any established power structure and avoided the forced loyalties and liabilities that tribal and religious affiliation might have entailed. For example, warriors drawn from Berber or Arab tribes might be expected to be loyal to their tribal leaders and to their lineages rather than to the caliphs. If a commander rose up against the caliph, it was often tricky to punish him without precipitating vengeance from his kin.

Saqaliba (sing. *saqlabi*) were manumitted military slaves of Slavic origin (Halm 1996: 278-80). They began to play an important role in the central state in both al-Andalus and North Africa, particularly in the Fatimid state centred on what is now Tunisia in the century just before the formation of the caliphate. The slaves had usually been captured or purchased as children and raised in the households of the dynastic families. Even after they were set free, they remained in the role of clients (*mawla*) to their former master and patron for life. The *saqaliba* were essentially strangers who had no other status or loyalty in Andalusian society than as client to their Arab patron. Thus the Slavic clients were considered to be unconditionally loyal. *Saqaliba* were often hired originally as pages, and then moved up into military offices, in some cases leading military campaigns. Some *saqaliba* were castrated and charged with guarding the harems, overseers of palaces and storehouses. With the break-up of the Córdoba caliphate, a few *saqaliba* formed *taifa* states of their own along the Sharq al-Andalus, or eastern coast of Spain.

In the earliest years of Islam, particularly in the Mashriq, the main and probably the only way to enter Muslim society was through submission to an individual member of an Arab tribe as a *mawla*, or client, which involved conversion to Islam in the process (Fierro 1999). Within a century or so after the conquest, however, under the influence of Malikism, a growing sectarian movement in Islam more or less equivalent to Sunnism or Shi'ism, new converts were seen instead as clients of the Muslim community at large rather than of specific Arab tribes or individual Arab patrons. This branch of Islam stressed the importance of the *umma* or Muslim community as a whole over that of Arabic ethnic identity. The Umayyad dynasty actually benefited from this shift, because it meant that new converts would no longer be attached by ties of loyalty and dependency to Arab factions settled in the hinterlands. Thus the 'spontaneous conversion' of indigenous non-Muslims seems have become much more widespread in al-Andalus, and was in fact probably the principal form of conversion there. These converts were termed *musalima* or 'new Muslims'.

It is equally important to realize that Arabization was not limited to converts to Islam. Christian populations who remained in their faith adopted Arab language, styles of dress, and lifeways. In traditional historiography, the Christians in al-Andalus are termed *mozarabs*, a word of uncertain derivation, even as to whether it comes from Latin or Arabic, but which seems to signify 'almost Arab' or 'mixed Arab'. Chalmeta (1991) has pointed out that the first known use of the term is in a Latin text of 1024 from Léon. It may actually have a pejorative connotation applied by the Christian conquerors, implying Christians who had been collaborators with the Arabs, or who had become too much like Arabs. It may well be, in fact, that enculturation into Arab lifeways was one of the first steps toward subsequent conversion. Fierro (1998: 309-11) has argued that in the early years of al-Andalus, the term *muwallad* may have referred to non-Arabs who had adopted Arab ways, and only later came to denote those who had actually converted. In an often quoted phrase, Bulliet (1990: 131) suggested that 'In a sense, a convert first became a member of the Muslim community and later discovered or tried to discover, what it meant to be a Muslim.' In any case, the appearance of Arab-influenced material culture may not be a fool-proof signal of ethnicity or conversion to Islam.

Pottery and Islamization

Archaeologically, the adoption of Islamic lifeways in rural settings during the medieval period of the Iberian Peninsula appears to be signalled by the addition of a distinctive assemblage of glazed, polychrome food serving vessel forms – conical bowls, platters, pitchers, tureens – in the late ninth and the tenth centuries. Taken together, this assemblage seems to have formed an essential part of communal food service and hospitality associated with the adoption of Islamic lifeways. Although there is much more work to be done in establishing the chronology of this development on a region by region basis, the adoption of this suite of vessel forms appears to have occurred during the late ninth century at the earliest, and probably more commonly in the mid- to late tenth century. With the exception of a form called the *jarritas* (see below), these forms are almost always glazed, and were produced in urban workshops in cities such as Seville, Córdoba, Toledo, Valencia and Zaragoza, as well as in North Africa.

This table and serving assemblage consists of several distinctive forms (I will use the terminology introduced by Rosselló Bordoy 1978). Carinated conical or rounded plates and tureens (*ataifor*) were used to serve stews and cooked legumes and cereals. Small bowls were used to serve individual servings of soup. A long-necked bottle with a side handle called a *redoma* would have been used to dispense liquids such as olive oil. One or usually two-handled tankards (*jarritas*) seem to have been used for serving either hot or cold liquids to drink. A little less than half of the *jarritas* recovered at Alcaria Longa were sooted, indicating they had been heated in a fire. Although some glazed *jarritas* are known, the most common kind are plainware with painted designs. Their production appears to have been much more localized than glazewares, as is evidenced by considerable variation in fabric, vessel form, paint type and design motif. *Jarritas* in the eastern part of al-Andalus were painted with red slip-paint designs. Those from southern Portugal are usually painted with white slip paint designs. A distinctive partially glazed beaked ceramic lamp called the *candil*, with clear connections to the Islamic world in the eastern Mediterranean, also appears during the late ninth or early tenth century.

Glazed wares, sometimes using tin oxide as an opacifier, were first used experimentally in Basra, Iraq, in the first half of the eighth century, apparently as a innovation developed

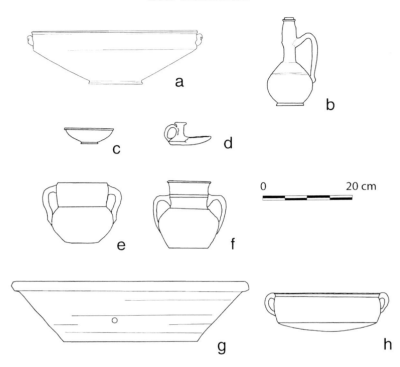

Fig. 5.2. A typical serving vessel and utilitarian pottery assemblage of the caliphal period. Glazed forms: (a) *ataifor*, (b) *redoma*, (c) small serving bowl, (d) *candil* or oil lamp. Plainware forms (e) and (f) *jarritas*; (g) *alguidar* or basin; (h) *cazuela*. These examples are all from Mértola or Alcaria Longa.

from a pre-Islamic opaque-glaze technology (Mason & Tite 1997). Over the course of the next century, an opaque-glaze technology was developed in Iraq and Egypt and subsequently spread to the rest of the Islamic world and also to Europe. In al-Andalus, the very earliest glazed pieces were monochrome light green or honey-coloured (*melado*) from the second half of the ninth century from sites like Pechina (see below) and El Zambo, a hilltop fortified site just west of Alicante (Gutiérrez Lloret 1996: 193). Mason and Tite argue that the two glaze colours are made with the same recipe, and draw colour from

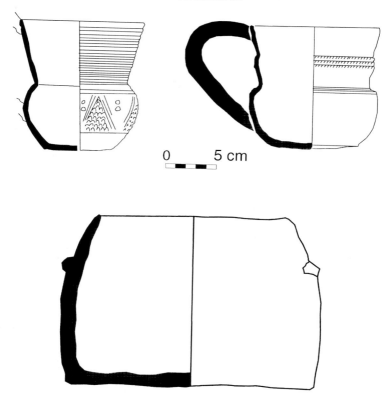

Fig. 5.3. Above, examples of the earliest glazed forms, showing orientalization of vessel forms, dating to the late emiral period – both are from Pechina/Bajjanah (redrawn from Guichard 2002: 84). Below, a typical slow-wheel produced *marmita*, or cooking pot, manufactured for regional distribution, dating to the emiral and early caliphal periods – from El Zambo (redrawn from Gutiérrez Lloret 1996: fig. 83).

iron present in the underlying paste: glazing inside and out produces a reducing atmosphere under the glaze, resulting in a green colour, while glazing on one side only is oxidizing, resulting in a reddish-tan or honey-coloured tint. The deep green glaze that appears in the late tenth and eleventh centuries was achieved with addition of copper oxide to the recipe.

This distinctively Islamic assemblage was superimposed over a regionally diverse array of utilitarian or common ware ceramic assemblages, which appear in many cases to have their roots in late Roman ceramic production and distribution systems. The most common forms in this category are cooking pots and water jars. A few new utilitarian forms were added to the ceramic assemblage in the emiral and caliphal periods. These include a *cazuela* used to fry meats, eggs and other foods, and a large thick-walled basin (*alcadafe* in Spanish, *alguidar* in Portuguese) used for washing and, in the case of large forms, for mixing bread dough (in traditional villages today, they are used for both). In contrast to the glazed food service forms, utilitarian wares show a considerable amount of local variation in form from area to area suggesting the formation of conservative local traditions in pottery production.

Ceramics and the state

Archaeologists have long theorized on how elites employ elaborate material objects to express and solidify – or materialize – power over their subject populations (DeMarrais et al. 1996). In the case of the Córdoba caliphate, this materialization strategy was unusually literal in the form of a specialized palatine ware called *verde y manganeso* which was manufactured at Madinat al-Zahra (Barceló 1997a; Escudero Aranda 1991; Rosselló Bordoy 1987). This ware, which came in several vessel forms, but most commonly in large conical plates (i.e. the *ataifor*), was typically glazed all over with a white tin glaze and decorated with green (copper oxide) and dark purple or black (manganese dioxide) designs. This glazed ware is thought to have been first manufactured in Egypt as early as the ninth century, spreading west into the Maghreb, and subsequently into al-Andalus during the mid-tenth century.

Many of the Madinat al-Zahra pieces carry inscriptions in stylized script, the most common of which is simply the term *al-mulk*, often repeated over and over again around the rim of a vessel. *Al-mulk* can be translated as 'royal power' or sovereignty – as the title of Surah 67 in the Quran it is often translated as 'the kingdom', as in the kingdom of God. In other contexts it translates as 'private property'. This message is found on other decorative objects produced at the palace, including textiles, ivory and bronze. Barceló points out a parallel use of the term on ceramic plates that probably date to the tenth-century Fatimid dynasty in Ifriqiya, or what is now Tunisia.

Following the extensive excavations at Madinat al-Zahra's outlying craft production areas during the 1970s, it was confirmed that this ware was manufactured at the palace complex itself. Later imitations of this glazed combination were manufactured elsewhere in al-Andalus, but are stylistically distinct. Rosselló Bordoy maintained that the wares were presented to various government agents from the outlying provinces as ambassadorial gifts from the caliph, in a manner similar to textiles (like the *tiraz*), or carved ivory boxes.

It is likely that elaborate glazed ceramics in general signal the extension of Córdoba's authority over communities in the hinterlands (Guichard 2002: 170). Hence glazed wares typically viewed as signals of Islamization may be more accurately viewed as 'caliphatization'.

Ceramics and Berberization

During the late seventh and eighth centuries, local production of wheel-thrown pottery in several parts of the Peninsula appears to have greatly diminished and in some regions disappeared altogether, a pattern that emerges around most of the Mediterranean during this period (Rautman 1998). In its place, handmade and slow-wheel made pottery industries appeared. Balfet (1965) and Peacock (1982) have argued that hand-formed pottery industries are usually household-based industries in which pottery is made by women primarily for household consumption. In contrast, wheel-thrown industries are usually located outside the household, where pottery is made by men primarily for sale in markets.

Traditional Berbers in North Africa have maintained a remarkably persistent and conservative tradition of household production of hand-formed ceramics (Balfet 1965; Redman & Myers 1981) for use in cooking and water storage. This has been shown to extend back in time to before the Roman occupation, as evidenced by hand-formed wares recovered at the Roman provincial capital of Volubilis, through the Arabization of the Maghreb, as evidenced by the occurrence of hand-formed wares at the early Islamic city of Basra (Benco 1987), and in later medieval Islamic levels of Qsar es-Seghir (Myers 1984). This tradition has survived several waves of modernization beginning as early as the eighteenth century (when, for example, the British style copper tea-pot was widely adopted). If North African Berbers tribes settled in rural Iberia during the Islamic period, one might expect that they would have brought with them the tradition of household production of hand-formed pottery.

The picture that is emerging, however, is much more complex. An excellent review of early Islamic period ceramic production technology and distribution in the southeastern Peninsula has been presented by Sonia Gutiérrez Lloret (1988; 1996: 31-70). Extensive studies of the late Roman and early emiral period (termed 'Paleoandalusí') sequence in southeastern Spain (Acién Almansa 1986, Acién Almansa and Martínez Madrid 1989; Gutiérrez Lloret 1988, 1996) have shown that by the end of the late Roman period, wheel-thrown pottery production had nearly ceased, and was only revived in the late ninth and the tenth centuries, during the consolidation of the Umayyad caliphate, perhaps as population densities had again increased and trade networks reformed to the point that such industries could be supported.

Gutiérrez Lloret finds that hand-formed pottery, which had constituted a important component of ceramic production here as in other parts of the Late Roman world, continues well into the first centuries after the Muslim invasions of 711. She sees this as a continuing response to relatively low levels of demand and to basic instabilities in the markets, rather than a sign of 'primitivism' or decadence. Hand-formed industries appear to be indicative of cultural continuity in indigenous populations, not immigrating Berbers. A clear example of cultural continuity with the late Roman period is the wide, shallow hand-formed plate that strongly resembles in profile previous forms in late *terra sigillata* or African Red Slipped wares (Gutiérrez Lloret 1996: 84). Another example is the flat-bottomed, incurving *marmita*, or cooking pot, that is found throughout the seventh century and probably back into the sixth (see Fig. 5.3, bottom). By the tenth century, this form is being produced on a slow wheel (*torno lento*, a wheel turned slowly by hand while hand-building the walls of the vessel), and the form is clearly being produced for regional markets. Similar forms are found throughout the western Mediterranean, including Sicily, Algeria (at Sétif), and Morocco (at Basra and Nakur). The production of slow-wheel made pottery for regional markets continues into the caliphal period.

The Islamic house as a signal of Islamization

Continuity and change in rural and urban house forms might reasonably be expected to signal ethnicity and religious beliefs in the archaeological record. The typical Islamic house consists of a walled compound with two to four long rectangular rooms opening onto an unroofed courtyard (detailed discussions of the medieval Islamic house are found in Bazzana 1992: 168-79, plates XCI to CIX; Fentress 1987; Redman 1986: 76-94). The entrance to the compound, which is often offset at a right angle, blocking view of the courtyard from the street, opens into the courtyard, and all the surrounding rooms are accessible only from there. Fentress makes the point that the courtyard actually contains the rooms, rather than in the case of the Roman atrium house, where rooms are built to enclose a courtyard. There is usually no access between the rooms themselves, which include sleeping rooms, rooms to entertain guests, and a kitchen. In urban contexts, houses usually have at least one latrine, which empties into a sewer under the street outside.

145

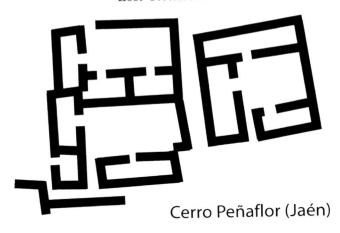

Cerro Peñaflor (Jaén)

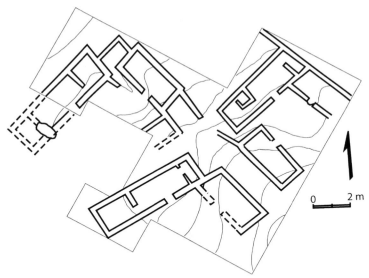

0   2 m

Alcaria Longa (Mértola)

Fig. 5.4. Rural house compounds showing Islamic courtyard house layout. Top: Cerro de Peñaflor (from Salvatierra Cuenca and Castillo Armenteros 1991); Bottom: Alcaria Longa (from author's files).

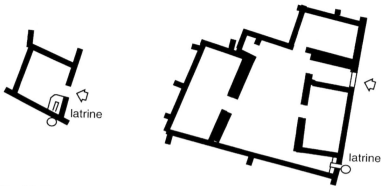

Fig. 5.5. House forms from Pechina/Bajjanah. Left, a one-room habitation with a latrine. Right, a typical Islamic courtyard house compound. Both date to the end of the emiral period or just after the establishment of the caliphate. Redrawn from Castillo Galdeano et al. 1987: plano 2.

This house form, with very little variation in spatial organization, is ubiquitous in urban housing in Islamic cities and towns by the ninth and tenth centuries, and is also common in some rural village contexts (see below). The size and degree of elaboration of such houses varies from large palaces to the humblest village abode. The source of this form has been the subject of some debate. Elizabeth Fentress (1987) provides a brief but useful summary of the problem as it stood in the late 1980s. Some argue that the courtyard house derives from the Hellenistic house by way of Sassanian influence on the development of Islamic architecture. North Africanists have argued for an *in situ* adoption of the form by Berber groups from Roman housing. Fentress concludes that the form existed in the nascent Arab world prior to Islam, may have had multiple origins, and was brought to the Maghreb and to al-Andalus with Islam. She also suggests that the spatial organization of the courtyard house was adapted to Muslim patriarchal family ideology. She argues that the defining characteristic of the form is the dominance of the courtyard over the rest of the building, which functions as a kind of *panopticon* from which the rest of the rooms and the activities within them can be easily observed and accessed. At the same time, the bent-axis entry to the whole compound protects the privacy of women's activities from outsiders. The Islamic patriarchal family, which is headed by the eldest male, is reflected in this spatial organization.

Fentress's study focuses on the medieval Islamic city of Sétif in Algeria, where Islamic style courtyard house compounds appear at the earliest by the late ninth or early tenth century. Courtyard house compounds appear in urban and rural village contexts in al-Andalus at about the same time, perhaps a little later. The earliest such compounds in urban contexts seem to coincide with the establishment of the Córdoba caliphate in 929, as in the urban site of Pechina/Bajjanah, discussed below. I am unaware of courtyard style houses dating any earlier in the Peninsula.

Courtyard houses also appear in rural village contexts, for example at Alcaria Longa and at the site of Cerro de Peñaflor (Salvatierra Cuenca & Castillo Armenteros 1991), in the Campiña de Jaén (see Chapter 3). Salvatierra and Castillo identify this settlement with the Berber settlement of al-Mallaha, or *alquería*, mentioned in the *Muqtabis*, a historical text of the *taifa* era historian Ibn Hayyan. Extensive excavations at the site of Cerro de Peñaflor revealed courtyard houses and a system of interconnected underground chambers carved into the bedrock that served as cisterns.

I have previously argued that the courtyard house compound in rural contexts constitutes evidence of Berber settlement in the rural hinterlands of Mértola in the Lower Alentejo of Portugal (Boone 1992; 1993), based on a strong resemblance to the 'Rifian courtyard' form described by Mikesell (1961: 74). These compounds have been dated to the period 950-1150 (Boone & Worman 2007). Salvatierra and Castillo's identification of the site of Cerro de Peñaflor with a historically documented Berber settlement would provide some support for this interpretation.

The Rifian courtyard house is found primarily in the region of northern Morocco occupied by the Aith Waryaghar, who, as I discussed in Chapter 3, were among the earliest Berber groups to be incorporated into an Islamic polity in the eighth century (assuming, of course, that the Waryaghar have historical continuity in the area back to that time). Myers (1979) and Redman et al. (1982) have argued that the Berber courtyard house is a rural permutation of the urban Islamic house form, introduced during the Islamization of the region in the eighth and ninth centuries. According to this argument, Berber groups would have already adopted the courtyard house style in northern Morocco and brought it with them to the Iberian Peninsula. However, the other possibility, and one which I now find more convincing, is that the Islamic style courtyard house was adopted in urban contexts in al-Andalus through direct influence from the East (although possibly by way of North Africa), and was subsequently adopted by rural villagers who may or may not have been of Berber origin. The mid-tenth- to eleventh-century dates for the rural forms, and the somewhat earlier tenth-century dates for courtyard houses in urban contexts, such as Pechina, discussed below, would argue in favour of this latter scenario, which is also more parsimonious.

It is very possible that the adoption of this house form is the result of multiple parallel and convergent sources, similar to the problem of the horseshoe arch, discussed at the beginning of this chapter. It also seems that the courtyard style house did not become established in Islamic culture until some time after the Arab conquest of the Maghreb and al-Andalus, probably in the late ninth or early tenth century, so it probably does not serve as a reliable chronological marker for Islamization or Arabization of indigenous populations in the eighth and ninth centuries. When the courtyard house form does appear, however, it appears to be strongly associated with the adoption of Islam.

Bajjanah

The emiral period site of Bajjanah (the present-day village of Pechina, Almería, Spain) is a good example of a Mediterranean urban port that served as an conduit for eastern Mediterranean architectural styles and craft industries into al-Andalus. Bajjanah is located on the Rio Andarax about 10 km from the river's mouth at the modern city of Almería (Castillo Galdeano & Martínez Madrid 1993; Castillo Galdeano et al. 1987). The Andarax is thought to have been a more or less permanent stream during classical and medieval times, and possibly navigable all the way up to Pechina. Mariner traders settled along the Mediterranean coast between Alicante and Aguilas had a long standing pattern, almost certainly dating back to the Late Roman period, of sailing to ports along the North African coast and wintering there, then returning to the Spanish coast in spring with cargoes of trade goods. They are said to have founded the coastal settlement of Tènes on the Algerian coast in 875. After the Arab invasion, these traders apparently formed a pact and established a semi-autonomous 'maritime republic'. Yemeni Arabs then settled in the area, having been charged with protecting the coast against Norse attacks by Abd al-Rahman II, following the attacks against the south coast, particularly Beja and Seville, in the mid-840s. In return, the Yemenis were granted irrigated lands in the Andarax valley. A watchtower called al-Mariyya was built at the river mouth, from which the modern toponym Almería is derived. As capital of a *kura*, or district under the emirate, Bajjanah grew rapidly from the Mediterranean trade, particularly with North Africa, as well as from agricultural production in the irrigated Andarax valley. A large mosque and fortification or rampart walls were said to have been constructed, reflecting the town's status as a *madinat*. After about forty years of independence, Bajjanah was peacefully incorporated into the nascent Umayyad caliphate in 922. In 955, the caliph Abd al-Rahman III moved the capital of the *kura* to Almería, probably as a response to threats to the coast from the expanding Fatimid dynasty, centred on Kairouan, near the old site of Carthage, in what is now Tunisia. Bajjanah then went into decline as a settlement, and by the early eleventh century was reported to be almost completely abandoned.

5. Islamization

As an Islamic settlement with well established historical dates in the emiral period, followed by decline and abandonment in the first few decades of the caliphate, Bajjanah offered an excellent opportunity for archaeological study of the early Islamic period, particularly with reference to questions concerning the pace and timing of Islamization. Excavations at the site of Bajjanah were undertaken between 1985 and 1988 under the direction of Manuel Acién Almansa and Francisco Castillo Galdeano.

Much of the original settlement is covered with the modern village of Pechina. An open area on the outskirts of the village was selected for excavation, and a contiguous area roughly 40 x 40 m was eventually opened, along with soundings and a long exploratory trench nearby. The excavations revealed a dense pattern of buildings in what may have been the edge of the *madina*.

Two clear stratigraphic levels were discerned in excavation. The earliest level (Level 1) contained mostly fill and wasters from nearby pottery kilns; no specific architectural features could be related to this deposition. None of the ceramics dated past the end of the emiral period. Level 2 above it was associated with the five houses that were excavated and the pottery kiln and glass foundry located nearby. This level contained green and black on white glazed wares – i.e. classic Madinat es-Zahra wares associated with the establishment of the Córdoba caliphate, as well as a higher proportion of glazed table wares in general. Level 2 contained a block of habitations and workshops located off a street that runs north-south from what is probably the centre of the settlement.

Five separate houses were revealed in Level 2, which corresponds to the period from the establishment of the Córdoba caliphate in 929 to the time of Bajjanah's decline and abandonment within a few decades after the capital of the *kura* was moved to Almería. In one case, a house had been divided into two separate domiciles during its use. Three of the houses were organized around patios, with kitchens, sleeping and living rooms arranged around an open, probably unroofed space 3-4 m wide and 3-7 m long. One of the patios had a cistern built into the floor. One of the patio houses had a stable attached. Plaster wainscoting in the patios was painted with ochre, and in some of sleeping rooms was covered with red and white checkerboard and triangular patterns.

The two smaller habitations consisted of a one-room structure about 3.3 x 3.3 m opening directly onto a small side street or alley, and a slightly larger house just across the alley, consisting of three successive rooms. The later house had been divided off from one of the larger patio houses discussed above. Castillo Galdeano et al. (1987) suggest that these small domiciles may have doubled as workshops for craft industry workers.

All five house structures, large and small, contained a latrine which drained through an exterior wall and into a small 'septic tank' in a street or alley outside. Bajjanah seems to have lacked an underground sewage drainage system, usually found in Islamic *madinas* of the period. In the patio houses, the latrines were in separated rooms with red plastered floors and the vestiges of red wall paintings. In the two smaller houses, the latrines were simply located in the corner of a room.

In the south corner of the excavations, a small portion of a cemetery was located in what was then an open area on the edge of the settlement. Eight skeletons were uncovered, oriented northeast-southwest, and facing southeast, the direction of Mecca. Owing to the proximity of the cemetery to habitations and workshops, and the lack of a clear delimiting wall around it, the excavators argue that the cemetery must date to a period after the active occupation of the room blocks just to the north, when this section of the settlement had been abandoned.

Conclusions

The term Islamization would, on the face of it, seem to refer to a process by which Islam is introduced to and adopted by a non-Muslim population. However, as it is used in reference to cultural change after the Arab conquest of Hispania, the meaning is more akin to that associated with 'Romanization' – the adoption of elite Roman lifeways, values and material culture in the Roman colonies. Investigators often attempt to make a distinction between Islamization and Arabization, and sometimes even Berberization in talking about material culture change during the formation of al-Andalus, but, other than obvious examples such as the appearance of mosques in place of churches, such a distinction remains very difficult to discern in the archaeological record itself, or even at the conceptual level. The association between being Arab and being a Muslim was very strong during the first century or two of the Arab empire. Since Arab culture was the prestige culture in al-Andalus, the pressure, or at least the temptation, to adopt Arab traits must have continued to be very strong even among those who did not convert. As was pointed out above, Arabization might well have been the first stage of conversion, at a point at which it was important to signal to others in the community where one's sympathies actually lay. Hence separating the various processes of change archaeologically may prove very difficult.

6

The transformation of
the year 929

Over the past three chapters we have seen that the many of the far-reaching changes in material culture associated with Arab and Berber conquest and settlement and with the process of Islamization occurred mainly in the first half of the tenth century, coinciding with the establishment of the Córdoba caliphate in 929, rather than with the initial Arab conquest in 711 two hundred years earlier. Part of the reason for this is that many of the elaborate architectural forms and craft industries that are commonly associated with Islamic civilization did not exist at the time of the conquest, as the Arab empire was still in its formative stages in the seventh and eighth centuries. Equally important was the fact that the economy and the fiscal and administrative infrastructure of al-Andalus during the emiral period lacked the strength and stability to generate the revenues necessary to support the intensive urban craft industries and construction that would flourish once the caliphate was established. Nor was the number of urban aristocratic consumers large enough to create the demand needed to stimulate urban craft production, elaborate construction, long-distance trade, and so on. Hence, while the conquest of 711 certainly constitutes a significant rupture in terms of political history, it could be argued that the real transformation occurs in the first few decades of the tenth century with the consolidation of caliphal power: what we might call 'caliphatization'. Put another way, an archaeologist lacking documentary evidence would be hard put to discern that a momentous event had occurred in 711. Her attention might be drawn instead to the explosive growth of Córdoba, the establishment of Madinat al-Zahra, the rapid spread of urban-based craft industries across the Peninsula, and the appearance of the castle/village (or *hisn/qarya*) in the early tenth century. I want to begin my concluding remarks by suggesting that looking at the formation of al-Andalus in archaeological perspective puts the continuity vs. rupture issue that I introduced in the first chapter in a different light.

The model of the medieval transition on which I have based much of my discussion, as originated by the work of Chris Wickham, is a gradualist model characterized by change along a continuum that runs between a centralized, tax-based state and a decentralized, land and rent-based society founded on dependency relations between landowners and cultivators. I have argued that this model's relevance continues even after the Arab conquest of Hispania, following up Wickham's suggestion that there is more continuity than difference between the Visigothic and the emiral period (2005: 41). As I argued in Chapter 4, this is more a case of parallel and convergent development than actual historical continuity, resulting from the fact that both the Visigothic and the Arab systems of surplus extraction had a more or less common heritage in the late Roman systems of taxation.

However, by the late ninth and early tenth centuries, the gradualist transition model starts to break down. In northern and western Europe, the pattern is one of an ever-weakening state culminating in a near complete decentralization of power among local and regional lords (Francovich & Hodges 2003: 106-14). In direct contrast, the formation of al-Andalus culminated in the emergence in 929 of a highly centralized Middle Eastern-style polity, complete with an aloof, nearly invisible but all-powerful caliph installed in a separate, self-sufficient palace complex, a vast bureaucracy and military built out of slaves, all centred around one of the largest cities in the world at the time. Two more opposite end results can hardly be imagined.

There are, however, some parallels or similarities that we

might learn from. The first similarity is in the timing: the coeval appearance in the early to mid-tenth century of *incastellamento*, or the castle/village complex in Latin Christian Europe and in al-Andalus, which, as I argued in Chapter 4, is unlikely to be a mere coincidence. In Europe, this development signals the final culmination of feudalism. In al-Andalus, it appears to signal the tension between local and regional interests in the hinterlands and the ultimately successful attempts by the Córdoba emirate to bring them under fiscal control. The second similarity is in the parallel factors of causation: both transformations were preceded by long periods of slow but sustained demographic and economic growth extending back into the beginning of the eighth century, capped by a period of rapid, transformative change. Long build-up followed by rapid transformation: here the utility of the gradualist model begins to fail us. What is needed is a model that accounts for transformation.

I want to suggest that Guy Bois's *The Transformation of the Year 1000* (1992) may be of some use despite the fact that its argument is presented as an alternative to the Wickham transition model. Bois's main premise was that late antiquity, defined in terms of the survival of institutions such as the slavery mode of production, extended all the way into the tenth century, and that the beginning of the Middle Ages began with a transformative phase shift that occurred around the year 1000. His argument is based on five propositions regarding the character of the medieval transition on the Continent, using an intensive documentary study of the French village of Lournand, located just north of Mâcon, as a case study. In place of a long transition characterized by the slowly shifting balance between taxation and rent-collecting, Bois saw the transition as a long, slow buildup that ended in a rapid phase shift, or transformation, in the mid- to late tenth century. His first proposition, following in the footsteps of Pierre Bonnassie's (1991a) work on Catalonia, is that between the fifth and tenth centuries western Europe remains throughout a slave-based economy and society. By this he means specifically that the majority of the landed aristocracy extracted wealth from primary producers through slave labour, not through the collection of rents. The rest of the landscape was filled with small landowners who worked their own lands. Bois estimates that servile families made up a minimum of 15% of the population. Only on the largest landed estates, which are also the most prominent in the documentary record, do we see the practice of infeudation, which dominates medieval society after the eleventh century. This constitutes a major departure from Wickham's view of the transition, since for Wickham slaves are really serfs (2005: 230-1), and for Bois, serfs are really slaves. I will not attempt to resolve or reconcile this tricky issue here; in any case, there is no doubt that slavery and the slave trade from northeastern Europe and Sub-Saharan Africa was a significant element of the economy of Islamic civilization in Egypt, the Middle East, the Maghreb and al-Andalus well into the late historic period (Hopkins 1973: 81-5; Lombard 1975: 194-203) and that slavery was present in al-Andalus at least into the tenth century (Fierro 1998: 319-22).

This leads to Bois's second proposition regarding the medieval transition: that the class structure of late antique society remained for the most part fundamentally unchanged up to the eleventh century. It consisted of an aristocracy whose wealth was drawn from land and the slaves who worked it, and a community of free peasants who worked their own land. This class structure in turn implies a continued ruralization of society to the eleventh century, which leads to his third proposition, that trade was limited to the movement of food and utilitarian goods between town and countryside, and took the form of barter as much as or more than the exchange of cash throughout the period. The fourth proposition is that rather than being a period of decline and disintegration, late antiquity undergoes modest but sustained economic and demographic growth, long before feudalism becomes the dominant mode of organization at the turn of the eleventh century. Finally, the Frankish period ended in a rupture at around 1000 in which subinfeudation reorganized society from top to bottom in long chains of relationships of dependency from monarch to serf. The image that comes to mind is of a solution that gradually becomes supersaturated with the addition of more and more solute, until the introduction of a seed, like a particle of dust, or a sudden drop in temperature, catalyzes the crystallization process, which spreads throughout the solution almost instantaneously. Subinfeudation created innumerable gradations of status between lords and vassals, gradations that stimulated the consumption of sumptuary goods to distinguish one from another. This in turn created a new context for trade in non-essential goods, paid for with money, which further stimulated the growth of craft and service industries that concentrated in the new and growing towns and cities. These new reservoirs of demand in turn stimulated long-distance trade in precious materials. Within a few short decades, the High Middle Ages were up and running.

At this point, I want to return to the idea that what ties the two areas north and south of the Pyrenees together is a pattern of slow, sustained economic and demographic growth followed by a rapid episode of transformation. In Chapter 3, I showed that the population of al-Andalus nearly tripled from the time of the Arab conquest to the peak of the caliphal period in the 960s, about 250 years later. A similar growth spurt is observed in Europe north of the Pyrenees (Davis 1986), although possibly delayed by 75 to 100 years. There are some good reasons to think that this growth trend is at least partially exogenous to the establishment of Arab or Muslim in place of Visigothic or Christian dominion. The frequent plague outbreaks that began in the 540s ceased rather suddenly around 750 (Little 2007). The climate may have been improving in the Mediterranean with the approach of the Medieval Optimum which peaked in the eleventh century – recall that the Roman empire peaked during a similar optimum at the beginning of the first millennium (Greene 1986). The introduction of new cultigens and new irrigation techniques may have increased productivity and stimulated economic and population growth during the Islamic period, but Butzer et al. (1985) have argued that the difference between Roman and Islamic irrigation agrosystems is one of degree rather than kind. We have already seen that are more similarities between the taxation systems of the Visigoths and the Arabs than differences – it is possible that the Christians were taxed even more and more regularly under Muslim rule. So it is possible to argue that Iberia would have experienced growth and prosperity in the closing centuries of the first millennium regardless of who was in charge.

What then, made the difference? Some insight might be gained by extending the comparative range beyond the shores of Europe and into North Africa. In 909, the imam Abdullah al-Mahdi Billah pronounced the establishment of the first Shi'a state in the newly founded city of Mahdia, about 100 km south of what had been Carthage, in Tunisia (Brett 2001; Halm 1996). As a symbolic gesture of sovereignty and legitimacy, the Mahdi immediately initiated the striking of gold dinars. Twenty years later, Abd al-Rahman would announce the establishment of the independent caliphate in Córdoba and begin striking gold dinars in a similar symbolic gesture. The near contemporaneous establishment of these two competing polities on opposite sides of the western Mediterranean was no coincidence. The Guadalquivir valley and Ifriqya (modern-day Tunisia) were two extremely fertile and productive agricultural regions that had experienced economic and demographic growth in the preceding centuries. As such, they each constituted a reservoir of demand for sumptuary goods in their rapidly developing urban centres and became locked in competition over control of sources of gold far to the south in the Niger.

The question of the role of long-distance trade and the spread of Islam in the development of the Middle Ages is by now a well-worn, some would say worn-out, debate. In Henri Pirenne's view, the decline and ruralization of the West was the result of the interruption of long-distance trade through the Mediterranean precipitated by the expansion of the Arab empire, causing an eclipse of trade in sumptuary goods that fuelled the urban economy of the ancient world (see Hodges & Whitehouse 1983). This trade was reopened by the Crusaders,

159

paving the way for economic development in the High Middle Ages. Maurice Lombard (1947; 1975) argued just the opposite: moving precious metals, slaves and other goods from West Africa, across the Sahara and from al-Andalus to the eastern Mediterranean, Islamic civilization reopened long-distance trade that had declined along with the western Roman empire. The gold brought up from the Niger stimulated the European economy, bringing about the Renaissance. As Bois writes: 'Symmetrical [i.e. opposite] conclusions, but identical premises, that is, the same priority to the exogenous factor and the explanation of trade by trade' (1992: 74).

We can perhaps avoid this circularity by shifting the emphasis to demand. Long-distance trade taps the wealth of social and geographical islands of purchasing power (Brett 2001: 255; Hopkins 1973: 58). These 'islands' consist of widely separated groups of affluent customers who might make up a small minority of the total population, but possess the disposable wealth to support a market for expensive goods that are not locally available. Islamic states in the West developed out of prosperous market economies that existed in two such islands: one in the Guadalquivir river valley and the other in Ifriqiya, or what is now Tunisia. Although there is a long-standing debate over the matter, a strong argument could be made for the idea that the trans-Saharan trade in gold and slaves was the basis for the formation of the Umayyad and Fatimid caliphates in the West (Boone et al. 1990; Ennahid 2002; Guichard 1999; Lacoste 1974; Lombard 1947). Resolution of that debate, however, would be the subject of a different book.

Bibliography

Abad Casal, L., Gutiérrez Lloret, S., Sanz, R. 1998. *El Tolmo de minateda. Una historia de tres mil quinientos años.* Toledo: Junta de Comunidades de Castilla-La Mancha.

Acién Almansa M. 1986. Cerámica a torno lento en Bezmiliana. Cronología, tipos y difusión. In *I Congreso de Arqueología Medieval Española*, pp. 243-67. Huesca.

Acién Almansa, M. 1989. Poblamiento y fortificación en el sur de al Andalus. La formación de un país de Husun. In *III Congreso de Arqueología Medieval Española (III CAME)*, pp. 135-50. Oviedo: Universidade de Oviedo.

Acién Almansa, M. 1997. *Entre el feudalismo y el Islam: 'Umar Ibn Hafsun en los historiadores, en las fuentes y en la historia.* Jaén: Universidad de Jaén.

Acién Almansa, M. 1998. Settlement and fortification in southern al-Andalus: the formation of a land of *husun*. In *The formation of al-Andalus. Part 1: History and society*, ed. M. Marín, pp. 347-76. Aldershot: Ashgate Variorum.

Acién Almansa, M. 1999. Poblamiento indígena en al-Andalus e indicios del primer poblamiento Andalusí. *al-Qantara* 20: 47-64.

Acién Almansa M, Martínez Madrid R. 1989. Cerámica islámica arcaica del suroeste de al-Andalus. *Boletín de Arqueología Medieval* 3:123-35

Acién Almansa, M., Vallejo Triano, A. 1998. Urbanismo y estado islámico: de *Corduba* a *Qurtuba-Madinat al Zahra.* In *Genèse de la ville islamique en al-Andalus et au Maghreb occidental*, ed. P. Cressier, M. García-Arenal, pp. 107-36. Madrid: Casa de Velázquez.

Alarcão, J. 1988. *O domínio romano em Portugal.* Mem Martins, Portugal: Publicações Europa-Americana.

Antunes, M.T., Sidarus, A. 1993. Mais um quirate cunhado em Beja em nome de Ibn Qasi e Abu Talib al-Zuhri. *Arqueologia Medieval* 2: 221-4.

Arbeiter, A. 2000. Alegato por la riqueza del inventario monumental hispanovisigodo. In *Visigodos y omeyas: un debate entre la antiqüedade tardía y la alta edad media (Mérida, abril de 1999)*, ed. L. Caballero Zoreda, P. Mateus Cruz, pp. 249-64. Madrid: Consejo Superior de Investigacions Científicas.

Argemi Relat, M., Oliver Bruy, J., Soler Chic, G. 1993. Alcaria Ruiva (Alentejo): un assentament rural entre dues formacions socio-

Bibliography

econòmiques. In *IV Congreso de Arqueología Medieval Española*, pp. 435-42. Alicante: Asociacion Española de Arqueología Medieval.

Arjona Castro, A. 2004. Posible localización de los restos arqueológicos del Dar al-Tiraz (Casa de tiráz) en Córdoba musulmana. *Boletín de la Real Academia de Córdoba de Ciencias, Bellas Letras y Nobles Artes*: 137-46.

Arjona Castro, A., Frochoso Sánchez, R. 2002. Localización del lugar donde estuvo ubicada la casa de la moneda (Dar-Al-Sikka) en la Córdoba islámica. *Boletín de la Real Academia de Córdoba de Ciencias, Bellas Letras y Nobles Artes*: 181-98.

Azkarate Garai Olaun, A., Ripoll López, G., Souto, J.A. 2000. Algunas reflexiones personales sobre el simposio 'visigodos y omeyas'. In *Visigodos y omeyas: un debate entre la antiqüedade tardía y la alta edad media (Mérida, abril de 1999)*, ed. L. Caballero Zoreda, P. Mateus Cruz, pp. 457-9. Madrid: Consejo Superior de Investigaciones Científicas.

Azuar Ruiz, R. 1982. Una interpretacion del 'hisn' Musulman en el ambito rural. *Revista de Investigacion y Ensayos del Instituto de Estudios Alicantinos Excma. Diputacion Provincial de Alicante* II Epoca: 33-41.

Azuar Ruiz, R. 1989. *Denia islámica: arqueología y poblamiento*. Alicante: Instituto de Cultura 'Juan Gil-Albert'.

Balfet, H. 1965. Ethnographical observation in North Africa and archeological interpretation. In *Ceramics and Man*, ed. F. Matson, pp. 166-77. Chicago: Aldine.

Barceló, M. 1990. Vísperas de feudales. La sociedad de *Sharq al-Andalus* justo antes de la conquista catalana. In *España. Al-Andalus. Sefarad: síntesis y nuevas perspectivas*, ed. F Maíllo Salgado, pp. 99-112. Salamanca: Universidad de Salamanca.

Barceló, M. 1993. Quina arqueologia per al-Andalus? *Arqueologia Medieval* 2: 5-16.

Barceló, M. 1997a. *Al-Mulk,* el verde y el blanco. La vajilla califal omeya de Madinat Al-Zahra. In *La cerámica altomedieval en el sur de al-Andalus*, pp. 291-9. Granada: Universidad de Granada.

Barceló, M. 1997b. *El sol que salió por occidente*. Jaén: Publicaciones de la Universidad de Jaén.

Barceló, M. 1997c. Un estudio sobre la estructura fiscal y procedimientos contables del Emirato omeya de Córdoba (138-300/755-912) y del Califato (300-366/912-976). In *El sol que salió por occidente*, ed. M Barceló. Jaén: Publicaciones de la Universidad de Jaén.

Barceló, M. 1998. The manifest Caliph: Umayyad ceremony in Córdoba, or the staging of power. In *The Formation of al-Andalus. Part 1: History and society*, ed. M. Marín, pp. 425-56. Aldershot: Ashgate Variorum.

Bazzana, A. 1992. *Maisons d'al-Andalus: habitat médiéval et structures du peuplement dans l'Espagne orientale*. Madrid: Casa de Velázquez.

Bazzana, A., Guichard, P., Segura Marti, J.M. 1982. Du hisn musulman au castrum chrétien: le château de Perpunchet (Lorcha, Prov. de Alicante). *Melanges de la Casa de Velázquez* 17: 449-65.

Bazzana, A., Cressier, P., Guichard, P. 1988. *Les châteaux ruraux d'al-*

Bibliography

Andalus: histoire et archéolgie des husun du sud-est de l'Espagne. Madrid: Casa de Velázquez.

Benco, N. 1987. *The early medieval pottery industry at al-Basra, Morocco.* Oxford: British Archaeological Reports.

Björkman, W. 1987. Maks. In *The Encyclopaedia of Islam,* 2nd edn, ed. C.E. Bosworth, E. van Donzel, W. Heinrichs, C. Pellat, pp. 194-5. Leiden: Brill.

Bois, G. 1992. *The transformation of the year 1000: The village of Lournand from antiquity to feudalism.* Manchester: Manchester University Press.

Bonnassie, P. 1991a. *From slavery to feudalism in south-western Europe.* Cambridge: Cambridge University Press.

Bonnassie P. 1991b. Society and mentalities in Visigothic Spain. In *From slavery to feudalism in south-western Europe,* pp. 60-103.

Boone, J.L. 1992. The first two seasons of excavations at Alcaria Longa. *Arqueologia Medieval* 2: 51-64.

Boone, J.L. 1993. The third season of excavations at Alcaria Longa. *Arqueologia Medieval* 3: 51-64.

Boone, J.L. 1994. Rural settlement and Islamization: the evidence from Alcaria Longa. In *Arqueologia en el entorno del bajo Guadiana: Actas del encuentro de arqueologia del suroeste,* ed. J.M. Campos, J.A. Pérez, F. Gómez, pp. 527-44. Huelva: Universidad de Huelva.

Boone J.L. 1996. Uma sociedade tribal no Baixo Alentejo medieval? *Arqueologia Medieval* 4: 25-35.

Boone J.L., Myers, J.E., Redman, C.L. 1990. Archeological and historical approaches to complex societies: the Islamic states of medieval Morocco. *American Anthropologist* 92: 630-45.

Boone J.L., Worman, F.S. 2007. Rural settlement and soil erosion from the late Roman period through the medieval Islamic period in the Lower Alentejo of Portugal. *Journal of Field Archaeology* 32: 115-32.

Brett, M. 2001. *The rise of the Fatimids: The world of the Mediterranean and the Middle East in the fourth century of the hijra, tenth century CE.* Leiden: Brill.

Brown, P. 1971. *The world of late antiquity: AD 150-750.* New York: W.W. Norton & Company.

Brown, P. 1978. *The making of late antiquity.* Cambridge, MA: Harvard University Press.

Bulliet, R.W. 1979. *Conversion to Islam in the medieval period: An essay in quantitative history.* Cambridge, MA: Harvard University Press.

Bulliet, R.W. 1990. Conversion stories in early Islam. In *Conversion and continuity: Indigenous Christian communities in Islamic lands,* ed. M. Gervers, R.J. Bikhazi, pp. 89-101. Toronto: Pontifical Institute of Medieval Studies.

Butt, J. 2007. Spain's great divide. *Times Literary Supplement,* 3 August 2007, issue no. 5444: 5-8.

Butzer, K., Mateu, J.F., Butzer, E.K., Kraus, P. 1985. Irrigation agrosystems in eastern Spain: Roman or Islamic origins? *Annals of the Association of American Geographers* 75: 479-504.

Bibliography

Butzer, K., Butzer, E.K., Mateu, J.F. 1986. Medieval Muslim communities of the Sierra de Espadán, kingdom of Valencia. *Viator, Medieval and Renaissance Studies* 17: 339-413.

Caballero Zoreda, L. 1997. Observations on historiography and change from the sixth to tenth centuries in the north and west of the Iberian Peninsula. In *The archaeology of Iberia: The dynamics of change*, ed. M. Diaz-Andreu, S. Keay, pp. 211-34. London: Routledge.

Caballero Zoreda, L. 2000. La architectura denominada de época visigoda: es realmente tardoromana o prerománico? In *Visigodos y omeyas: un debate entre la antiqüedade tardía y la alta edad media (Mérida, abril de 1999)*, ed. L. Caballero Zoreda, P. Mateus Cruz, pp. 207-48. Madrid: Consejo Superior de Investigaciones Científicas.

Cahen, C. 1953. L'évolution de l'iqta' du XIè au XIIIè siècle. *Annales, E.S.C.* 8: 25-52.

Castillo Galdeano, F., Martínez Madrid, R. 1993. Producciones cerámicas en Bayyana. In *La cerámica altomedieval en el sur de al-Andalus*, ed. A. Malpica Cuello, pp. 67-116. Granada: Universidad de Granada.

Castillo Galdeano, F., Martínez Madrid, R., Acién Almansa, M. 1987. Urbanismo e industria en Bayyana. Pechina (Almería). In *II Congreso de Arqueología Medieval Española*, pp. 538-48. Madrid.

Catlos, B. 2004. *The victors and the vanquished: Christians and Muslims of Catalonia and Aragon, 1050-1300*. Cambridge: Cambridge University Press.

Chalmeta P. 1991. Mozarab. In *The Encyclopaedia of Islam*, 2nd edn, ed. C.E. Bosworth, E. van Donzel, W. Heinrichs, C. Pellat, pp. 246-9. Leiden: Brill.

Chalmeta, P. 1992. Muwallad. In *The Encyclopaedia of Islam*, 2nd edn, ed. C.E. Bosworth, E. van Donzel, W. Heinrichs, C. Pellat, pp. 807-8. Leiden: Brill.

Chalmeta, P. 1994a. An approximate picture of the economy of al-Andalus. In *The legacy of Muslim Spain*, ed. S.K. Jayyusi, pp. 741-58. Leiden: Brill.

Chalmeta, P. 1994b. *Invasión e islamización: la sumisión y la formación de al-Andalus*. Madrid: Editorial MAPFRE.

Chavarría, A. 2005. Villas in Hispania during the fourth and fifth centuries. In *Hispania in late antiquity*, ed. M. Kulikowski, K. Bowes, pp. 519-55. Leiden: Brill.

Chavarría, A, Lewit, T. 2004. Archaeological research on the late antique countryside. In *Recent research on the late antique countryside*, ed. W. Bowden, L. Lavan, C. Machado, pp. 3-54. Leiden: Brill.

Collins, R. 1994. *The Arab conquest of Spain: 710-797*. Oxford: Blackwell.

Collins, R. 2004. *Visigothic Spain: 409-711*. London: Blackwell.

Correia, S., Oliveira, J.C. 1993. *Núcleo visigótico (Museu Regional de Beja): Catálogo*. Beja, Portugal: Museu Regional de Beja.

Cressier, P. 1991. Agua, fortificaciones, y poblamiento: el aportede la arqueología a los estudios sobre el sureste península. *Aragón en la edade media* 9: 403-27.

Bibliography

Cressier, P. 1992. *Estudios de arqueología medieval en Almería*. Granada: Ediciónes Instituto de Estudios Almerienses.

Cressier, P. 1998a. Observaciones sobre fortificación y minería en la Almería islámica. In *Castillos y territorio en Al-Andalus*, ed. A Malpica, pp. 470-96: Athos-Pérgamos.

Cressier, P. 1998b. Remarques sur la fonction de château islamique dans l'actuelle province d'Alméria, à partir des textes et de l'archeologie. In *'L'Incastellamento': Actes des recontres de Gérone (26-27 Novembre 1992) et de Rome (5-7 Mai 1994)*, ed. M. Barceló, P. Toubert, pp. 234-47. Rome: Ecole Française de Rome.

Cressier, P., García-Arenal, M. 1998. *Genèse de la ville islamique en al-Andalus et au Maghreb occidental*. Madrid: Casa de Velázquez, CSIC.

Crone, P. 1980. *Slaves on horses: The evolution of the Islamic polity*. Cambridge: Cambridge University Press.

Crone, P. 1987. *Meccan trade and the rise of Islam*. Princeton: Princeton University Press.

Crone, P. 2003. *Preindustrial societies: Anatomy of the pre-modern world*. Oxford: Oneworld.

Cunliffe, B. 1993. *Wessex to AD 1000*. London: Longman.

Davis, D.E. 1986. Regulation of human population in northern France and adjacent lands in the Middle Ages. *Human Ecology* 14: 245-59.

DeMarrais, E., Castillo L.J., Earle, T. 1996. Ideology, materialization, and power strategies. *Current Anthropology* 37: 15-31.

Dewald, E.T. 1922. The appearance of the horseshoe arch in Western Europe. *American Journal of Archaeology* 26: 316-37.

Díaz, P.C. 2000. City and territory in Hispania in late antiquity. In *Towns and their territories between late antiquity and the early middle ages*, ed. G.P. Brogiolo, N. Gauthier, N. Christie, pp. 3-36. Leiden: Brill.

Edwards J. 2001. The changing use of worship in Roman and medieval Córdoba. In *The destruction and conservation of cultural property*, ed. R. Layton, J. Thomas, P.G. Stone, pp. 221-35. London: Routledge.

Ennahid, S. 2002. *Political economy and settlement systems of medieval northern Morocco, BAR S1059*. Oxford: Archaeopress.

Escudero Aranda, J. 1991. Producciones cerámicas en Madinat al-Zahra: la cerámica 'verde y manganeso'. *Cuadernos de Madinat al-Zahra* 2: 127-61.

Fabian, J.F., Santonja Gomez, M., Fernandez Moyano, A., Benet, N. 1986. Los poblados hispano-visigodos de 'Cañal', Pelayos (Salamanca). In *Actas del I Congreso de Arqueología Medieval Española* (CAME I), pp. 187-202. Zaragoza: Diputación General de Aragón. Departamento de Cultura y Educación.

Fentress, E. 1987. The house of the Prophet: North African Islamic housing. *Archeologia Medievale* 14: 47-68.

Fierro, M. 1995a. Árabes, beréberes, muladíes y mawali. Algunas reflexiones sobre los datos de los diccionarios biográficos andalusies. *Estudios Onomástico-Biográficaos de al-Andalus* VIII: 269-344.

Bibliography

Fierro, M. 1995b. Cuatro preguntas en torno a Ibn Hafsun. *Al-Qantara* 16: 221-57.

Fierro, M. 1998. Four questions in connection with Ibn Hafsun. In *The Formation of al-Andalus. Part 1: History and Society*, ed. M. Marín, pp. 291-345. Aldershot: Ashgate Variorum.

Fierro, M. 1999. Los *mawali* de Abd al-Rahman I. *Al-Qantara* 20: 65-97.

Fierro, M. 2005. *Abd al-Rahman III: The first Cordoban caliph*. Oxford: Oneworld.

Francovich, R., Hodges, R. 2003. *Villa to village: The transformation of the Roman countryside in Italy, c. 400-1000*. London: Duckworth.

Garen, S. 1992. Santa María de Melque and church construction under Muslim rule. *Journal of the Society of Architectural Historians* 51: 288-305.

Glick, T.F. 1979. *Islamic and Christian Spain in the early middle ages: Comparative perspectives on social and cultural formation*. Princeton: Princeton University Press.

Glick, T.F. 1995. *From Muslim fortress to Christian castle: Social and cultural change in medieval Spain*. Manchester: Manchester University Press.

Goffart, W. 1980. *Barbarians and Romans, A.D. 418-584: The techniques of accommodation*. Princeton: Princeton University Press.

Goffart, W. 2006. *Barbarian tides: The migration age and the later Roman empire*. Philadelphia: University of Pennsylvania Press.

Goitein, S.D. 1965. The exchange rate of gold and silver money in Fatimid and Ayyubid times: a preliminary study of the relevant Geniza material. *Journal of Economic and Social History of the Orient* 8:1-46.

Goodrich, D.R. 1978. *A 'Sufi' revolt in Portugal: Ibn Qasi and his 'Khitab Khal' al-Na'Layn'*. Ann Arbor: University Microfilms International.

Goody, J. 1984. *The development of the family and marriage in Europe*. Cambridge: Cambridge University Press.

Gorges, J.-G. 1979. *Les villas hispano-romaines*. Paris: E. de Broccard.

Greene, K. 1986. *The archaeology of the Roman economy*. London: B.T. Batsford.

Guichard, P. 1969. Le peuplement de la région de Valence aux deux premiers siècles de la domination musulmane. *Mélanges de la Casa Velázquez* 5: 103-56.

Guichard, P. 1974. Les arabes ont bien envahi l'Espagne: les structures sociales de l'Espagne musulmane. *Annales, E.S.C.* 29: 1483-513.

Guichard, P. 1976. *Al-Andalus: estructura antropológica de una sociedade islámica en occidente*. Barcelona: Barral Editories.

Guichard, P. 1994. The social history of Muslim Spain. In *The legacy of Muslim Spain*, ed. S.K. Jayyusi, pp. 679-708. Leiden: Brill.

Guichard, P. 1995. *La España musulmana: al-Andalus omeya (siglos VII-XI)*. Madrid: Ediciones Temas de Hoy.

Guichard, P. 1998. The population of the region of Valencia during the first two centuries of Muslim domination. In *The formation of al-Andalus.*

Bibliography

Part 1: History and society, ed. M. Marín, pp. 129-82. Aldershot: Ashgate Variorum.

Guichard, P. 1999. Omeyyades et Fatimides au Maghreb. Problematique d'un conflit politico-idealogique (vers 929-980). In *L'Egypte fatimide: son art et son histoire*, ed. M. Barrucand, pp. 55-67. Paris: Presses de l'Université de Paris-Sorbonne.

Guichard, P. 2002. *De la expansión Árabe a la Reconquista: esplendor y fragiladad de al-Andalus*. Granada: Fundación El Legado Andalusí.

Gutiérrez Lloret S. 1988. *Cerámica común paleoandalusí del sur de Alicante (Siglos VII-X)*. Alicante: Caja de Ahorros Provincial de Alicante.

Gutiérrez Lloret, S. 1989. Espacio y poblamiento paleoandalusí en el sur de Alicante: origen y distribución. *III Congreso de Arqueología Medieval Española*, pp. 341-8. Oviedo.

Gutiérrez Lloret, S. 1996. *La cora de Tudmir de la antigüedad tardía al mundo islámico: poblamiento y cultural material*. Madrid-Alicante: Casa de Velázquez-Diputación Provincial de Alicante.

Gutiérrez Lloret, S. 1998a. Eastern Spain in the sixth century in the light of archaeology. In *The sixth century: production, distribution and demand*, ed. R. Hodges, W. Bowden, pp. 161-84. Leiden: Brill.

Gutiérrez Lloret, S. 1998b. From *civitas* to *madina*: destruction and formation of the city in southeast al-andalus – the archaeological debate. In *The formation of al-Andalus. Part 1: History and society*, ed. M. Marín, pp. 217-64. Aldershot: Ashgate Variorum.

Gutiérrez Lloret, S. 2000. Algunas consideraciones de la cultura material de las época visigoda y emiral en el territorio de Tudmir. In *Visigodos y omeyas: un debate entre la antiqüedade tardía y la alta edad media (Mérida, abril de 1999)*, ed. L. Caballero Zoreda, P. Mateus Cruz, pp. 95-116. Madrid: Consejo Superior de Investigaciones Científicas.

Gutiérrez Lloret, S., Abad Casal, L., Gamo Parras, B. 2004. La iglesia visigoda de El Tolmo de Minateda (Hellín, Albacete). *Antigüedad y cristianismo* 21: 137-69.

Halm, H. 1996. *The empire of the Mahdi: The rise of the Fatimids*. Leiden: Brill.

Halm, H. 1998. Al-Andalus and Gothica Sors. In *The formation of al-Andalus, Part 1: History and society*, ed. M. Marín, pp. 39-50. Aldershot: Ashgate Variorum.

Hart, D.M. 1976. *The Aith Waryaghar of the Moroccan Rif: An ethnography and history*. Tucson, Arizona: University of Arizona Press.

Heather, P. 1992. The emergence of the Visigothic kingdom. In *Fifth-century Gaul: A crisis of identity?*, ed. J. Drinkwater, H. Elton, pp. 84-94. Cambridge: Cambridge University Press.

Heather, P. 1996. *The Goths*. Oxford: Blackwell Publishing.

Hillgarth, J.N. 1985. Spanish historiography and Iberian reality. *History and Theory* 24: 23-43.

Hodges, R., Whitehouse, D. 1983. *Mohammed, Charlemagne and the origins of Europe*. London: Duckworth.

Hopkins, A.G. 1973. *An economic history of West Africa*. London: Longman.

Bibliography

Hopkins, J.F.P. 1958. *Medieval Muslim government in medieval Barbary.* London: Luzac & Co. Ltd.

Izquierdo Benito, R. 1994. *Excavaciones en la ciudad hispanomusulmana de Vascos (Navalmoralejo, Toledo): Campañas 1983-1988.* Toledo: Servicio de Publicaciones de l Junta de Comunidades de Castilla-La Mancha.

Izquierdo Benito, R. 1999. *Vascos: La vida cotidiana en una ciudad fronteriza de al-Andalus.* Toledo: Junta de Comunidades de Castilla-La Mancha.

James, E. 1979. Cemeteries and the problem of Frankish settlement in Gaul. In *Names, words and graves: Early medieval settlement*, ed. P.H. Sawyer. Leeds: School of History University of Leeds.

Kamen, H. 2007. *The disinherited: Exile and the making of Spanish culture 1492-1975.* New York: Harper Collins.

Keay, S. 1988. *Roman Spain.* London: University of California Press.

Kennedy, H. 1996. *Muslim Spain and Portugal: A political history of al-Andalus.* London: Longman.

Kennedy, H. 1998. From antiquity to Islam in the cities of al-Andalus and al-Mashriq. In *Genèse de la ville islamique en al-Andalus et au Maghreb occidental*, ed. P. Cressier, M. García-Arenal, pp. 53-64. Madrid: Casa de Velázquez.

Koder, J. 1996. Climatic change in the fifth and sixth centuries? In *The sixth century: End or beginning?*, ed. P. Allen, E. Jeffreys, pp. 270-86. Brisbane: Australian Association for Byzantine Studies.

Kouznetsov, V., Lebedynsky, L. 2005. *Les Alains: cavaliers des steppes, seigneurs du Caucase.* Paris: Éditions Errance.

Kulikowski, M. 2007. Plague in Spanish late antiquity. In *Plague and the end of antiquity: The pandemic of 541-750*, ed. L.K. Little, pp. 150-70. Cambridge: Cambridge University Press.

Kuper, A. 1982. Lineage theory: a critical retrospect. *Annual Review of Anthropology* 11: 71-95.

Kuper, A. 1988. *The invention of primitive society: Transformation of an illusion.* London: Routledge.

Lacoste, Y. 1974. The general characteristics and fundamental structures of medieval North African society. *Economy and Society* 3:1-17.

Larsen, L.B. 2008. New ice core evidence for a volcanic cause of the A.D. 536 dust veil. *Geophysical Research Letters* 35: L04708.

Little, L.K., ed. 2007. *Plague and the end of antiquity: The pandemic of 541-750.* Cambridge: Cambridge University Press.

Lombard, M. 1947. L'or musulman du VII au XI siècles. *Annales, Economies, Sociétés* 2: 143-60.

Lombard, M. 1975. *The golden age of Islam.* New York: Elsevier.

Lopes, M.C., Alfenim, R. 1994. A villa Romana do Monte da Cegonha. In *Arqueologia en el entorno del Bajo Guadiana: Actas del encuentro de arqueologia del suroeste*, ed. J.M. Campos, J.A. Pérez, F. Gómez, pp. 485-502. Huelva: Universidade de Huelva.

Lopes, V. 2003. *Mértola na antiguidade tardia: A topografia histórica da*

Bibliography

cidade e do seu território nos alvores do cristianismo. Porto: Gráfica Maiadouro.

Macías, S. 1993. Um espaço funerário. In *Basilica Paleocristã*, ed. C. Torres, S. Macias, pp. 30-57. Mértola: Campo Arqueológico de Mértola.

Manzano Moreno, E. 1991. *La frontera de al-Andalus en época de los omeyas*. Madrid: Consejo Superiior de Investigaciones Científicas.

Manzano Moreno, E. 1998. The settlement and organization of the Syrian *junds* in al-Andalus. In *The formation of al-Andalus. Part 1: History and society*, ed. M. Marín, pp. 85-114. Aldershot: Ashgate Variorum.

Manzano Moreno, E. 2006. *Conquistadores, emires y califas: Los omeyas y la formación de al-Andalus*. Barcelona: Crítica.

Martín Viso, I. 2006. Central places and the territorial organization of communities: the occupation of hilltop sites in early medieval northern Castile. In *People and space in the Middle Ages, 300-1300*, ed. W. Davies, G. Halsall, A. Reynolds, pp. 167-86. Turnhout: Brepols.

Martínez Enamorado V. 1997. *Un espacio de frontera. Fortalezas medievales de los valles del Guadalteba y del Turón*. Málaga: Universidad de Málaga.

Martínez Enamorado, V. 1996. Algunas consideraciones espaciales y toponímicas sobre Bobastro. *al-Qantara* 27: 59-77.

Martínez Enamorado, V. 2003. *Al-Andalus desde la periferia. La formación de una sociedad musulmana en tierras malagueñas (siglos VII-X)*. Málaga: Servicio de Publicaciones: Centro de Ediciones de la Diputación de Málaga (CEDMA).

Martínez Enamorado, V. 2004. Sobre las 'cuidadas iglesias' de Ibn Hafsun. Estudio de la basílica hallada in la ciudad de Bobastro (Ardales, Málaga). *Madrider Mitteilungen* 45: 507-31.

Martínez Enamorado, V. in press. Fatimid ambassadors in Bobastro? Changing religious and political allegiances in the Islamic West. *Journal of the Economic and Social History of the Orient*.

Mason, R.B., Tite, M.S. 1997. The beginnings of tin opacification of pottery glazes. *Archaeometry* 39: 41-58.

Matos, L. 1994. Cerro da Vila. In *Arqueologia en el entorno del bajo Guadiana: Actas del encuentro de arqueologia del suroeste*, ed. J.M. Campos, J.A. Pérez, F. Gómez, pp. 521-5. Huelva: Universidad de Huelva.

Menocal, M.R. 2002. *Ornament of the world*. New York: Little, Brown and Company.

Mikesell, M.W. 1961. *Northern Morocco: A cultural geography*. Berkeley: University of California Press.

Munson, H. 1989. On the irrelevance of the segmentary lineage model in the Moroccan Rif. *American Anthropologist* 91: 386-400.

Murphy, R., Kasdan, L. 1959. The structure of parallel cousin marriage. *American Anthropologist* 61: 17-29.

Myers, J.E. 1979. *Ethno-archaeology of a Moroccan Village: Architecture, artifacts and activities*. Master's thesis. Binghamton: State University of New York at Binghamton.

Myers, J.E. 1984. *The political economy of ceramic production: A study of*

Bibliography

the Islamic commonware pottery of medieval Qsar es-Seghir. PhD dissertation, State University of New York, Binghamton. Ann Arbor, Michigan: University Microfilms, Inc.

Navarro, E.J., Centelles Izquierdo, F.X. 1986. El yacimiento de epoca visigoda del Pla de Nadal (Riba-Roja de Turia, Camp de Turia; Valencia. In *Actas del I Congreso de Arqueología Medieval Española (CAME I)*, pp. 25-40. Zaragoza: Diputación General de Aragón. Departamento de Cultura y Educación.

Olmo Enciso, L. 1992. El reino visigodo de Toledo y los territorios bizantinos. Datos sobre la heterogeneidad de la 'Península Iberica. In *Colloquio Hispano-Italiano de Arqueologia Medieval*, pp. 185-98. Granda: Patronato de la Alhambra y Generalife.

Palol, P. 1966. Demografía y arqueología hispánica. Siglos IV-VIII. Ensayo de cartografía. *Boletín de Seminario de Arte y Arqueología* 32: 5-67.

Peacock, D.P.S. 1982. *Pottery in the Roman world: An ethnoarchaeological approach*. London: Longman.

Pellat, C. 1992. Nakur. In *The Encyclopaedia of Islam*. 2nd edn, ed. C.E. Bosworth, E. van Donzel, W. Heinrichs, C. Pellat, pp. 941-3. Leiden: Brill.

Pettengill, J.S. 1979. The impact of military technology on European income distribution. *Journal of Interdisciplinary History* 10: 201-25.

Pohl, W., Reimitz, H., eds 1998. *Strategies of distinction: The construction of ethnic communities, 300-800*. Leiden: Brill.

Randsborg, K., ed. 1989. *The birth of Europe: Archaeology and social development in the first millennium A.D.*, vol. 16. L'Erma di Bretschneider.

Rautman, M. 1998. Handmade pottery and social change: the view from late Roman Cyprus. *Journal of Mediterrranean Archaeology* 11: 81-104.

Redman, C.L. 1986. *Qsar es-Seghir, an archeological view of medieval life*. New York: Academic Press.

Redman, C.L., Myers, J.E. 1981. Interpretation, classification and ceramic production: a medieval North African case study. In *Production and distribution: A ceramic viewpoint*, ed. H. Howard, E.L. Morris, pp. 285-307.

Redman, C.L., Boone, J.L., Myers, J.E. 1982. Fourth season of excavations at Qsar es-Seghir. *Bulletin d'Archeologie Marocaine* 2:263-87.

Reinhardt, W. 1945. Sobre el asentamiento de los visigodos en la peninsula. *Archivo Espanol de Arqueología* 18: 124-39.

Reynolds, P. 1993. *Settlement and pottery in the Vinalopó valley (Alicante, Spain) A.D. 400-700*. Oxford: Tempvs Reparatvm.

Reynolds, P. 2005. Hispania in the late Roman Mediterranean: ceramics and trade. In *Hispania in Late Antiquity*, ed. M. Kulikowski, K. Bowes, pp. 369-486. Leiden: Brill.

Ripoll López, G. 1985. *La necrópolis visigoda de El Carpio de Tajo (Toledo)*. Madrid: Ministerio de Cultura.

Ripoll López, G. 1998. The arrival of the Visigoths in Hispania: population problems and the process of acculturation. In *Strategies of distinction: The construction of ethnic communities, 300-800*, ed. W. Pohl, H. Reimitz. Leiden: Brill.

Bibliography

Ripoll López, G. 1999. The transformation and process of acculturation in late antique Hispania: select aspects from urban and rural archaeological documentation. In *The Visigoths: Studies in culture and society*, ed. A. Ferreiro, pp. 263-302. Leiden: Brill.

Ripoll López, G., Arce, J. 2000. The transformation and end of Roman *villae* in the West (fourth-seventh centuries): problems and perspectives. In *Towns and their Territories Between Late Antiquity and the Early Middle Ages*, ed. G.P. Brogiolo, N. Gauthier, N. Christie, pp. 63-114. Leiden: Brill.

Ripoll López, G., Velázquez, I. 1995. *La Hispania visigoda: Del rey Ataúlfo a Don Rodrigo*. Madrid: Ediciones Temas de Hoy.

Rosselló Bordoy, G. 1978. *Ensayo de sistematizacion de la cerámica arabe en Mallorca*. Palma de Mallorca.

Rosselló Bordoy, G. 1987. Algunas observaciones sobre la decoración cerámica en verde manganeso. *Cuadernos de Madinat al-Zahra* 1: 125-37.

Safran, J.M. 2000. *The second Umayyad caliphate: The articulation of caliphal legitimacy in al-Andalus*. Cambridge: Harvard University Press.

Sahlins, M. 1961. The segmentary lineage: an organization of predatory expansion. *American Anthropologist* 63: 322-45.

Salvatierra Cuenca, V. 1993. Las cerámicas precalifales de la cora de Jaén. In *La cerámica altomedieval en el sur de al-Andalus*, ed. A. Malpica Cuello, pp. 239-58. Granada: Universidad de Granada.

Salvatierra Cuenca, V. 1997. The origins of al-Andalus (eighth and ninth centuries): continuity and change. In *The archaeology of Iberia: The dynamics of change*, ed. M. Diaz-Andreu, S. Keay, pp. 265-78. London: Routledge.

Salvatierra Cuenca, V., Castillo Armenteros, J.C. 1991. El poblamiento rural: Histórico o intemporal? El case del Arroyo del Salado, Jaén. *Cuadernos de Madinat al-Zahra* 3: 47-75.

Salvatierra Cuenca, V., Serrano Peña, J.L., Pérez Martínez, M.C. 1998. La formación de la ciudad en al-Andalus. Elementos para una nueva propuesta. In *Genèse de la ville islamique en al-Andalus et au Maghreb occidental*, ed. P. Cressier, M. García-Arenal, pp. 185-206. Madrid: Casa de Velázquez.

Scales, P. 1994. *The fall of the caliphate of Córdoba: Berbers and andalusis in conflict*. Leiden: Brill.

Scales, P. 1997. Córdoba under the Umayyads: A 'Syrian' garden city? In *Urbanism in medieval Europe: Papers of the Medieval Europe Brugge Conference*, ed. G. De Boe, F. Verbaeghe, pp. 175-82. Zellik: Doornveld.

Simonsen, J.B. 1988. *Studies in the genesis and early development of the caliphal taxation system*. Copenhagen: Akademisk Forlag.

Taha, A.D. 1989. *The Muslim conquest and settlement of North Africa and Spain*. London: Routledge and Kegan Paul.

Thompson, E.A. 1982. *Romans and barbarians: The decline of the Western empire*. Madison: University of Wisconsin Press.

Bibliography

Torres Balbás, L. 1998. Cities founded by the Muslims in al-Andalus. In *The formation of al-Andalus. Part 1: History and society*, ed. M. Marín, pp. 265-89. Aldershot: Ashgate Variorum.

Torres, C., Macías, S. 1993. *Museu de Mértola: Basilica paleocristã*. Mértola: Campo Arqueológico de Mértola.

Toubert, P. 1973. *Les structures du Latium médiéval: le Latium méridional et la Sabine du IX siècle à la fin du XIIe siècle*. Rome: Ecole Française de Rome.

Toubert. P. 1990. *Castillos, señores, y campesinos en la Italia medieval*. Barcelona: Critica.

Velázquez Soriano, I. 2001. *Documentos de época visigoda escritos en pizarra, siglos VI-VIII*. Turnhout: Brepols,

Ward-Perkins, B. 2005. *The fall of Rome and the end of civilization*. Oxford; New York: Oxford University Press.

Wasserstein, D.J. 2002. Inventing tradition and constructing identity: the genealogy of 'Umar ibn Hafsun between Christianity and Islam. *al-Qantara* 22: 269-97.

Wasserstein, D.T. 1985. *The rise and fall of the party-kings: Politics and society in Islamic Spain 1002-1086*. Princeton: Princeton University Press.

Wickham, C. 1984. The other transition: from the ancient world to feudalism. *Past and Present* 103: 3-36

Wickham, C. 1985. The uniqueness of the East. *Journal of Peasant Studies* 12: 166-96.

Wickham, C. 2005. *Framing the early middle ages: Europe and the Mediterranean 400-800*. Oxford: Oxford University Press.

Wolfram, H. 1987. *History of the Goths*. Berkeley: University of California Press.

Index

Index